A Treasury of
LOVE
POEMS

Collected, Arranged
and Introduced by
RODNEY DALE

• BOOK • BLOCKS •

Acknowledgements

Rodney Dale thanks Charlotte Edwards
for bringing together his selection of
poems, and Antony Gray for a design that
enhances their sense. For permission
to include works, we are indebted to
John Arthur and Peter Scupham.

Contents

On Love, and its Poetry

On Love, and its Poetry

> . . . And let's be truly thankful
> For the chemical reactions
> That make us fall in love.

Love is perhaps the most elusive of the emotions. It's unlikely that you will feel grief, joy, envy or any other emotion without some clear reason, and I feel pretty sure that my grief or joy or whatever feels much the same to me as yours does to you. But love often strikes without reason. It can hit you as love at first sight – across a crowded room, on some enchanted evening . . . the song puts it so well, as songs do – or it may creep up on you like a thief in the night and steal your heart away. Equally, it can evaporate for no apparent reason, leaving you wondering what brought it on in the first place, puzzled that its subject could ever have had that effect on you.

As an interpersonal emotion, love is ethereal, inexplicable, fugitive. So trying to capture it in words is some challenge. A unique emotion demands a unique means of expression; thus so many writers turn to verse, for in verse you can use less usual – or even completely new – words, and constructions, unsuited to prose. The conventions of verse provide an admirable medium for those who would attempt to capture love. And, apart from allowing 'poetic' language and expression, the medium may also give structure to the poet's thoughts. The rhythm and the rhyme-scheme may help to shape, pace and control the development of the original idea, and it is interesting to look at a finished poem to see how its structure might have informed the detail of what is being said.

In *The Stuffed Owl**, we are invited to smile at a couplet allegedly written by 'A Young Tradesman Poet':

---

* An anthology of bad verse selected by D B Wyndham Lewis and Charles Lee (London 1930)

No more will I endure love's pleasing pain,
Nor round my heart's leg tie his galling chain.

But, clumsy as it may be; however inept its imagery; that couplet exemplifies the confusion of what the poet (or would-be poet) is trying to capture when he sets pen to paper. It echoes, perhaps, an attempt by 'A Young Secretary Poet' on whose shorthand pad I surreptitiously read on the London Underground many years ago:

I wish I knew how to tell you I love you. But there just isn't enough time, or enough words, in the whole world . . .

We who have been there know exactly what she's trying to say.

So what constitutes a love poem? Not all poems that mention love are love poems; not all love poems mention love. Many of the poems in this book are addressed to a specific person, with the writer rehearsing the qualities of his – or her – love; others are about love, or the qualities of love, or express the feeling of love, or the environment in which love develops. In short, all human love is here . . . and some non-human love too, for I have interpreted my brief quite liberally; thus I have included 'The Owl and the Pussy-Cat'. For that poem is a compendium of symbolic expressions of love. The Owl – presumably the male partner – accompanies himself on the guitar as he sings of his love beneath Addison's spacious firmament on high. The (female) Pussy-Cat proposes marriage – so it must be a leap-year – and then, 367 days later, having acquired the necessary annular token of eternity, they are married by a convenient turkey with an appropriate licence. After a simple but nourishing wedding-breakfast, they dance the night away hand in hand – wing in paw – in the moonlight. So, however curious the build-up, we are left with that timelessly eternal image of the ethereal moonlit dance of the newlyweds. It takes its place with the final sentence of *The House at Pooh Corner** – 'But wherever they go, and whatever

---

* A A Milne (London 1928)

happens to them on the way, in that enchanted place on the top of the Forest a little boy and his Bear will always be playing.'

What is love? At some point in the evolution of the animal kingdom, 'the chemical reactions' must have been augmented by (turned into) the feeling that we describe as 'falling in love' – 'whatever that means' as HRH The Prince of Wales said in his oft-shown betrothal interview. And what *does* it mean? Where in the tree of evolution does a chemically-driven behaviour pattern become overlaid by the emotion that we call love, felt in the way that we feel it? Amoebae? Jellyfish? Flatworms?

Never mind the lower invertebrates; do Mr and Mrs Lion fall in love? It may be the chemical reactions that draw them together, but we surely know – thanks to Sir David Attenborough and his colleagues – that there is some other force strong enough to hold them together as a couple, year after year, till death do them part. When a lion in the jungle gives a great big roar there's another lion who knows just what he's roaring for.

Human love 'as we know it' has been around for a very long time. Writings throughout the ages show that, although the environment in which emotions are experienced has altered out of all recognition, the emotions themselves have not. Would anyone doubt that the feeling of frustration is the same for a prehistoric craftsman with a blunt axe as for a commuter learning that the 8.24 has been cancelled? Or that the reaction of a witness to a jobsworth falling into a stagnant pool has not changed since slime immemorial? By the same token, feelings of love have remained unchanged over the millennia. But since we must accept that, at bottom, all emotions are due to chemical reactions, one wouldn't expect them to have changed – and here's a collection of love poems to prove it.

RODNEY DALE
Haddenham, Cambridgeshire, May 2003

WILLIAM LANGLAND (*c.*1330–*c.*1400)

1 Love Is the Treacle of Sin

Truth telleth thee that love is the treacle of sin,
A sovran salve for body and soul.
Love is the plant of peace, most precious of the virtues.
Heaven could not hold it, so heavy was love,
Till it has of this earth eaten its fill;
Then never lighter was a leaf upon a linden tree,
Than love was when it took the flesh and blood of man.
Fluttering, piercing as a needle's point,
No armour may it stay, nor no high walls.

2   *To His Wife*

'Petually
Constrained am I
With weeping eye
   To mourn and 'plain,

That we so nigh
Of progeny
So suddenly
   Should part in twain.

When ye are gone
Comfort is none,
But all alone
   Endure must I.

With grievly grone
Making my mone,
As it were one
 That should needs die.

What chance I suddein
So doth me stay'n
In every way'n
 That for no thing

I cannot lay'n,
Nor yet refrain
Mine eyes twain
 From sore weeping!

3   *To Mistress Anne*

Mistress Anne,
I am your man,
As you may well espy.
If you will be
Content with me,
I am your man.

But if you will
Keep company still
With every knave that comes by,
Then you will be
Forsaken of me,
That', am your man.

But if you fain,
I tell you plain,
That I presently shall die,

I will not such
As loves too much,
That am your man.

For if you can
Love every man
That can flatter and lie,
Then are ye
No match for me,
That am your man.

For I will not take
No such kind of make
(May all full well it trie!),
But off will ye cast
At any blast,
That am your man.

4 To *Mistress Margery Wentworth*

With margerain gentle,
　The flower of goodlihead,
Embroidered the mantle
　Is of your maidenhead.
Plainly I cannot glose;
　Ye be, as I devine,
The pretty primrose,
　The goodly columbine.
With margerain gentle,
　The flower of goodlihead,
Embroidered the mantle
　Is of your maidenhead.
Benign, courteous, and meek
　With wordés well devised;
In you, who list to seek,
　Be virtues well comprised.

With margerain gentle,
   The flower of goodlihead,
Embroidered the mantle
   Is of your maidenhead.

5 *To My Lady, Elizabeth Howard*

To be your remembrancer, madam, I am bound,
   Like to Irene, maidenly of port,
Of virtue and conning the well and perfect ground;
   Whom Dame Nature, as well I may report,
   Hath freshly embeautied with many a goodly sort
Of womanly features, whose flourishing tender age
Is lusty to look on, pleasant, demure, and sage.

6   *To My Lady, Mirrel Howard*

My little lady I may not leave behind,
   But do her service needs now I must;
Benign, courteous, of gentle heart and mind,
   Whom Fortune and Fate plainly have dicust
   Long to enjoy pleasure, delight, and lust:
The embudded blossoms of roses red of hue,
With lillies white your beauty doth renew.

Compare you I may to Cydippe, the maid,
   That of Acontius, when she found the bill
In her bosom, lord, how she was afraid!
   The ruddy shame-facedness in her visage fill,
Which manner of abashment became her not ill!
Right so, madam, the roses red of hue
With lillies white your beauty doth renew.

7 *Farewell, Love*

Farewell, Love, and all thy laws forever.
  Thy baited hooks shall tangle me no more.
  Senec and Plato call me from thy lore
To perfect wealth my wit for to endeavour.
In blind error when I did persever,
  Thy sharp repulse, that pricketh ay so sore,
  Hath taught me to set in trifles no store
And scape forth since liberty is lever.
Therefore farewell. Go trouble younger hearts
  And in me claim no more authority.
  With idle youth go use thy property
And thereon spend thy many brittle darts:
  For hitherto though I have lost all my time,
  Me lusteth no longer rotten boughs to climb.

8   The Lover Laments the Death of His Love

The pillar perished is whereto I leant,
The strongest stay of mine unquiet mind:
The like of it no man again can find,
From east to west still seeking though he went
To mine unhap for hap away hath rent

Of all my joy the very bark and rind,
And I, alas, by chance am thus assigned
Daily to mourn till death do it relent.
But since that thus it is by destiny,
What can I more but have a woeful heart,
My pen in plaint, my voice in careful cry,
My mind in woe, my body full of smart.
And I myself, myself always to hate,
Till dreadful death do ease my doleful state?

9   Quondam Was I

Quondam was I in my lady's grace,
    I think as well as now be you:
And when that you have trod the trace,
    Then shall you know my words be true,
That *quondam* was I.

Quondam was I. She said, 'for ever'.
    That 'ever' lasted but a short while,
A promise made not to dissever;
    I thought she laughed, she did but smile.
Then *quondam* was I.

Quondam was I that full oft lay
    In her arms with kisses many a one.
It is enough that I may say,
    Though 'mong the moe now I be gone,
Yet *quondam* was I.

Quondam was I: she will you tell
    That since the hour she was first born
She never loved none half so well
    As you. But what though she had sworn,
Sure *quondam* was I.

10 *Stealing a Kiss*

Alas! madam, for stealing of a kiss,
   Have I so much your mind then offended?
Have I then done so grievously amiss,
   That by no means it may be amended?
Then revenge you, and the next way is this.
   Another kiss shall have my life ended.
For to my mouth the first my heart did suck,
The next shall clean out of my breast it pluck.

11   *A Vow to Love Faithfully*
howsoever He Be Rewarded

Set me whereas the sun doth parch the green,
Or where his beams do not dissolve the ice,
In temperate heat, where he is felt, and seen,
In presence pressed of people, mad or wise;
Set me in high, or yet in low degree,
In longest night, or in the shortest day;

In clearest sky, or where clouds thickest be,
In lusty youth, or when my hairs are grey:
Set me in heaven, in earth, or else in hell,
In hill, or dale, or in the foaming flood;
Thrall, or at large, alive whereso I dwell,
Sick, or in health, in evil fame or good;
Hers will I be, and only with this thought,
Content myself, although my chance be nought.

12   When Raging Love

When raging love with extreme pain
   Most cruelly distrains my heart,
When that my tears, as floods of rain,
   Bear witness of my woeful smart;
     When sighs have wasted so my breath
     That I lie at the point of death,

I call to mind the navy great
   That the Greeks brought to Troye town,
And how the boistous winds did beat
   Their ships, and rent their sails adown;
     Till Agamemnon's daughter's blood
     Appeased the gods that them withstood.

And how that in those ten years' war
   Full many a bloody deed was done,
And many a lord that came full far
   There caught his bane, alas, too soon;
     And many a good knight overrun,
     Before the Greeks had Helen won.

Then think I thus: sith such repair,
   So long time war of valiant men,
Was all to win a lady fair,
   Shall I not learn to suffer then,
     And think my life well spent to be,
     Serving a worthier wight than she?

JOHN HARINGTON (?–1582)

13   The Heart of Stone

Whence comes my love? O heart, disclose!
It was from cheeks that shame the rose,
From lips that spoil the ruby's praise,
From eyes that mock the diamond's blaze:
Whence comes my woe? as freely own;
Ah me! 'twas from a heart like stone.

The blushing cheek speaks modest mind,
The lips befitting words most kind,
The eye does tempt to love's desire,
And seems to say, ' 'Tis Cupid's fire';
Yet all so fair but speak my moan,
Since nought doth say the heart of stone

Why thus, my love, so kind bespeak
Sweet eye, sweet lip, sweet blushing cheek, –
Yet not a heart to save my pain?
O Venus, take thy gifts again!
Make not so fair to cause our moan,
Or make a heart that's like your own.

14 *Husband to Wife*

If duty, wife, lead thee to deem
    That trade most fit I hold most dear,
First, God regard, next me esteem,
    Our children then respect thou near.

Our house both sweet and cleanly see,
    Order our fare, thy maids keep short;
Thy mirth with mean well mixed be;
    Thy courteous parts in chaste wise sort.

In sober weed thee cleanly dress;
    When joys me raise, thy cares down cast;
When griefs me seize, thy solace cease;
    Whoso me friend, friend them as fast.

In peace give place, whatso I say;
    Apart complain, if cause thou find;
Let liberal lips no trust betray,
    Nor jealous humour pain thy mind.

If I thee wrong, thy griefs, unfold;
    If thou me vex, thine error graunt;
To seek strange toils be not too bold;
    The strifeless bed no jars may haunt.

Small sleep and early prayer intend;
    The idle life, as poison, hate;
No credit light nor much speech spend;
    In open place no cause debate.

No thwarts, no frowns, no grudge, no strife;
    Eschew the bad, embrace the best;
To troth of word join honest life,
    And in my bosom build thy nest.

15   *Wife to Husband*

Husband, if you will be my dear,
   Your other self you must -me make;
So, next to God, you shall be near;
   So, of our babes, care will I take.

An wholesome house and strong-built, give;
   See needful things be never scace;
Provide your men unidly live.
   Use courteous speech, show friendly face.

T'observe your times, if time I choose,
   To know my time you must take pain;
And how your friends you would I use,
   So, look my friends you entertain.

Your storms for stubborn servants stay,
    And gently warn me in mine ear;
As you may at Your pleasure play,
    So, when I sport, he not severe.

That I you please, doth not alone
    In all respects myself suffice;
For good, of moe, I would you known,
    And long from home staved in nowise.

If no suspicions rise, you read
    Suspicious cause, t'eschew were best;
Whatever care the day doth breed,
    Agree, the night yield pleasant rest.

Whatso, a wooer, you me behight,
    Now, husband good, perform as due;
Penelop's path if I hold right,
    Ulysses' steps see you tread true.

16   *On Monsieur's Departure*

I grieve and dare not show my discontent,
I love and yet am forced to seem to hate,
I do, yet dare not say I ever meant,
I seem stark mute but inwardly do prate.
  I am and not, I freeze and yet am burned,
  Since from myself another self I turned.

My care is like my shadow in the sun,
Follows me flying, flies when I pursue it,
Stands and lies by me, doth what I have done.
His too familiar care doth make me rue it.
  No means I find to rid him from my breast,
  Till by the end of things it be supprest.

Some gentler passion slide into my mind,
For I am soft and made of melting snow;
Or be more cruel, love, and so be kind.
Let me or float or sink, be high or low.
　Or let me live with some more sweet content.
　Or die and so forget what love ere meant.

17   *The Fire of Love*

The fire of love in youthful blood
Like what is kindled in brushwood,
   But for a moment burns,
Yet, in that moment, makes a mighty noise:
It crackles, and to vapour turns,
   And soon itself destroys,

But, when crept into aged veins,
It slowly bums, and long remains,
   And, with a silent heat,
Like fire in logs, it glows and warms 'em long!
And tho' the flame be not so great,
   Yet is the heat as strong.

NICHOLAS BRETON (c.1545–c.1626)

18   A Country Song

In the merry month of May,
In a morn by break of day,
Forth I walked by the wood side,
Whereas May was in his pride.
There I spied all alone
Phyllida and Corydon.
Much ado there was, God wot,
He would love and she would not.
She said, never man was true;
He said, none was false to you.
He said, he had loved her long;
She said, love should have no wrong.
Corydon would kiss her then;
She said, maids must kiss no men,
Till they did for good and all.
Then she made the shepherd call

All the heavens to witness truth,
Never loved a younger youth.
Thus with many a pretty oath,
Yea and nay, and faith and troth,
Such as silly shepherds use,
When they will not love abuse,
Love, which had been long deluded,
Was with kisses sweet concluded:
And Phyllida with garlands gay
Was made the Lady of May.

EDWARD DE VERE, EARL OF OXFORD (1550–1604)

19 *A Court Lady Addresses Her Lover*

Though I be strange, sweet friend, be thou not so;
   Do not annoy thyself with sullen will.
My heart hath vowed, although my tongue say no,
   To rest thine own, in friendly liking still.

Thou seest we live amongst the lynx's eyes,
   That pries and spies each privy thought of mind;
Thou knowest right well what sorrows may arise
   If once they chance my settled looks to find.

Content thyself that once I made an oath
   To shield myself in shroud of honest shame;
And when thou list, make trial of my troth,
   So that thou save the honour of my name.

And let me seem, although I be not coy,
    To cloak my sad conceits with smiling cheer;
Let not my gestures show wherein I joy,
    Nor by my looks let not my love appear.

We silly dames, that false suspect do fear,
    And live within the mouth of envy's lake,
Must in our hearts a secret meaning bear,
    Far from the show that outwardly we make.

So where I like, I list not vaunt my love;
    Where I desire, there must I feign debate.
One bath my hand, another bath my glove,
    But he my heart whom most I seem to hate.

Thus farewell, friend: I will continue strange;
    Thou shalt not hear by word or writing aught.
Let it suffice, my vow shall never change;
    As for the rest, I leave it to thy thought.

EDMUND SPENSER (*c.*1552–1599)

20   To His Love: *Mark when She Smiles*

Mark when she smiles with amiable cheer,
  And tell me whereto can ye liken it:
When one each eyelid sweetly do appear
  An hundred graces as in shade to sit.

Likest it seemeth in my simple wit
  Unto the fair sunshine in summer's day:
That when a dreadful storm away is flit,
  Through the broad world doth spread its goodly ray:

At sight whereof each bird that sits on spray,
  And every beast that to his den was fled
Comes forth afresh out of their late dismay,
  And to the light lift up their drooping head.

    So my storm-beaten heart likewise is cheered,
    With that sunshine when cloudy looks are cleared.

21 *To His Love: One Day I Wrote Her Name*

One day I wrote her name upon the strand,
  But came the waves and washed it away:
Again I wrote it with a second hand,
  But came the tide, and made my pains his prey.

Vain man, said she, that doest in vain assay
  A mortal thing so to immortalize,
For I myself shall like to this decay,
  And eek my name be wiped out likewise.

Not so (quoth I), let baser things devise
  To die in dust, but you shall live by fame:
My verse your virtues rare shall eternize,
  And in my heavens write your glorious name.

    Where whenas Death shall all the world subdue,
    Our love shall live, and later life renew.

22 *O Mighty Charm!*

Trust not the treason of those smiling looks.
   Until ye have their guileful trains well tried!
For they are like but unto golden hooks,
   That from the foolish fish their baits do hide:

So she with flattering smiles weak hearts doth guide
   Unto her love, and tempt to their decay;
Whom, being caught, she kills with cruel pride,
   And feeds at pleasure on the wretched prey.

Yet even whilst her bloody hands them slay,
   Her eyes look lovely, and upon them smile,
That they take pleasure in their cruel play,
   And, dying, do themselves of pain beguile.

    O mighty charms which makes men love their bane,
    And think they die with pleasure, live with pain.

23   *Like Truthless Dreams*

Like truthless dreams, so are my joys expired,
  And past return are all my dandled days;
My love misled, and fancy quite retired,
  Of all which past, the sorrow only stays.

My lost delights, now clean from sight of land,
  Have left me all alone in unknown ways;
My mind to woe, my life in fortune's hand,
  Of all which past, the sorrow only stays.

As in a country strange without companion,
  I only wail the wrong of death's delays,
Whose sweet spring spent, whose summer well nigh
                        done,
  Of all which past, the sorrow only stays;

    Whom care forewarns, ere age and winter cold,
    To haste me hence, to find my fortune's fold.

24

Praised Be Diana's Fair and Harmless Light

Praised be Diana's fair and harmless light,
    Praised be the dews, wherewith she moists the ground,
Praised be her beams, the glory of the night,
    Praised be her power, by which all powers abound.

Praised be her nymphs, with whom she decks the woods,
    Praised be her knights, in whom true honour lives,
Praised be that force, by which she moves the floods;
    Let that Diana shine, which all these gives.

In heaven Queen she is among the spheres,
    In ay she mistress-like makes all things pure,
Eternity in her oft change she bears,
    She beauty is, by her the fair endure.

25   *My True Love Hath My Heart*

My true love hath my heart and I have his,
By just exchange one for another given.
I hold his dear, and mine he cannot miss;
There never was a better bargain driven.
My true love hath my heart and I have his.

His heart in me keeps him and me in one,
My heart in him his thoughts and senses guides;
He loves my heart, for once it was his own;
I cherish his, because in me it bides.
My true love hath my heart and I have his.

26   Sonnet: Because I breathe

Because I breathe not love to every one,
   Nor do not use set colours for to wear,
   Nor nourish special locks of vowed hair,
Nor give each speech a full point of a groan,
The courtly nymphs, acquainted with the moan
   Of them, who in their lips love's standard bear:
   'What, he?' say they of me, 'now I dare swear,
He cannot love; no, no, let him alone.'

And think so still, so Stella know my mind.
   Profess indeed I do not Cupid's art;
But you fair maids, at length this true shall find,
   That his right badge is but worn in the heart;
     Dumb swans, not chattering pies, do lovers prove;
     They love indeed, who quake to say they love.

27 *Sonnet: On Cupid's Bow*

On Cupid's bow how are my heart-strings bent,
  That see my wrack, and yet embrace the same!
  When most I glory, then I feel most shame:
I willing run, yet while I run, repent.
My best wits still their own disgrace invent;
  My very ink turns straight to Stella's name;
  And yet my words, as them my pen doth frame,
Avise themselves that they are vainly spent.

For though she pass all things, yet what is all
That unto me, who fare like him that both
  Looks to the skies, and in a ditch doth fall?
O let me prop my mind, yet in his growth,
    And not in nature for best fruits unfit.
    'Scholar,' saith Love, 'bend hitherward your wit.'

28 *Apollo Speaks*

FROM *Midas*

My Daphne's hair is twisted gold,
Bright stars a-piece her eyes do hold,
My Daphne's brow enthrones the Graces,
My Daphne's beauty stains all faces,
On Daphne's cheek grow rose and cherry,
On Daphne's lip a sweeter berry;
Daphne's snowy hand but touched does melt,
And then no heavenlier warmth is felt;
My Daphne's voice tunes all the spheres,
My Daphne's music charms all ears.
Fond am I thus to sing her praise;
These glories now are turned to bays.

29 *Apelles Speaks*

FROM *Campaspe*

Cupid and my Campaspe played
At cards for kisses; Cupid paid.
He stakes his quiver, bow and arrows,
His mother's doves and team of sparrows,
Loses them too; then down he throws
The coral of his lip, the rose
Growing on 's cheek (but none knows how),
With these the crystal of his brow,
And then the dimple of his chin:
All these did my Campaspe win.
At last he set her both his eyes;
She won, and Cupid blind did rise.
O Love! has she done this to thee?
What shall, alas, become of me?

30   *What Thing Is Love?*

What thing is love? for sure love is a thing.
It is a prick, it is a sting,
It is a pretty, pretty thing;
   It is a fire, it is a coal,
   Whose flame creeps in at every hole;
And as my wit doth best devise,
Love's dwelling is in ladies' eyes,
   From whence do glance love's piercing darts,
   That make such holes into our hearts;
And all the world herein accord,
Love is a great and mighty lord;
   And when he list to mount so high,
   With Venus he in heaven doth lie,
And evermore hath been a god,
Since Mars and she played even and odd.

31 *Love Guards the Roses of Thy Lips*

Love guards the roses of thy lips
   And flies about them like a bee;
If I approach he forward skips,
   And if I kiss he stingeth me.

Love in thine eyes doth build his bower,
   And sleeps within their pretty shine;
And if I look the boy will lour,
   And from their orbs shoots shafts divine.

Love works thy heart within his fire,
   And in my tears doth firm the same;
And if I tempt it will retire,
   And of my plaints doth make a game.

Love, let me cull her choicest flowers;
    And pity me, and calm her eye;
Make soft her heart, dissolve her lours.,
    Then will I praise thy deity.

But if thou do not, Love, I'll truly serve her,
In spite of thee, and by firm faith deserve her.

32   Love in My Bosom Like a Bee

Love in my bosom like a bee
   Doth suck his sweet;
Now with his wings he plays with me,
   Now with his feet.
Within mine eyes he makes his nest,
His bed amidst my tender breast;
My kisses are his daily feast,
And yet he robs me of my rest.
   Ah, wanton, will ye?

And if I sleep, then percheth he
   With pretty flight,
And makes his pillow of my knee
   The livelong night.
Strike I my lute, he tunes the string;
He music plays if so I sing;
He lends me every lovely thing;

Yet cruel he my heart doth sting.
  Whist, wanton, still ye!

Else I with roses every day
  Will whip you hence,
And bind you, when you long to play,
  For your offence.
I'll shut mine eyes to keep you in,
I'll make you fast it for your sin,
I'll count your power not worth a pin.
Alas! what hereby shall I win
  If he gainsay me?

What if I beat the wanton boy
  With many a rod?
He will repay me with annoy,
  Because a god.
Then sit thou safely on my knee,
And let thy bower my bosom be;
Lurk in mine eyes, I like of thee.
O Cupid, so thou pity me,
  Spare not, but play thee!

33 *Diaphenia Like the Daffodowndilly*

Diaphenia like the daffodowndilly,
White as the sun, fair as the lily,
   Heigh ho, how I do love thee!
I do love thee as my lambs
Are belovèd of their dams.
   How blest were I if thou would'st prove me!

Diaphenia like the spreading roses,
That in thy sweets all sweets encloses,
   Fair sweet, how I do love thee!
I do love thee as each flower
Loves the sun's life-giving power.
   For, dead, thy breath to life might move me.

Diaphenia like to all things blessèd,
When all thy praises are expressèd,
  Dear joy, how I do love thee!
As the birds do love the spring,
Or the bees their careful king.
  Then in requite, sweet virgin, love me!

MICHAEL DRAYTON (1563–1631)

34   Give Me Myself

You're not alone when you are still alone:
   O God, from you that I could private be!
Since you one were, I never since was one,
   Since you in me, my self since out of me.

Transported from myself into your being,
   Though either distant, present yet to either;
Senseless with too much joy, each other seeing,
   And only absent when we are together.

Give me my self, and take your self again!
   Devise some means but how I may forsake you!
So much is mine that doth with you remain,
   That taking what is mine, with me I take you.

     You do bewitch me! O that I could fly
     From my self you, or from your own self I!

35   *My Heart Was Slain*

My heart was slain, and none but you and I;
   Who should I think the murder should commit?
Since but yourself there was no creature by,
   But only I; guiltless of murd'ring it.
It slew itself, the verdict on the view

   Do quit the dead, and me not accessory:
Well, well, I fear it will be proved by you,
   The evidence so great a proof doth carry.
But O, see, see, we need inquire no further,

   Upon your lips the scarlet drops are found,
And in your eye the boy that did the murder,
   Your cheeks yet pale, since first he gave the wound,
     By this I see, however things be past,
     Yet heaven will still have murder out at last.

36   *To His Coy Love*

I pray thee, leave, love me no more,
    Call home the heart you gave me!
I but in vain that saint adore
    That can but will not save me.
These poor half-kisses kill me quite –
    Was ever man thus served:
Amidst an ocean of delight
    For pleasure to be staryèd!

Show me no more those snowy breasts
    With azure riverets branched,
Where, whilst mine eye with plenty feasts,
    Yet is my thirst not stanchèd;
O Tantalus, thy pains ne'er tells
    By me thou art prevented:
'Tis nothing to be plagued in hell,
    But thus in heaven tormented.

Clip me no more in those dear arms,
    Nor thy life's comfort call me,
O these are but too powerful charms,
    And do but more enthral me!
But see how patient I am grown
    In all this coil about thee:
Come, nice thing, let my heart alone,
    I cannot live without thee!

37   Since There's No Help

Since there's no help, come, let us kiss and part,
  Nay, I have done; you get no more of me;
And I am glad, yea, glad with all my heart,
  That thus so cleanly I myself can free.

Shake hands for ever; cancel all our vows;
  And when we meet at any time again,
Be it not seen in either of our brows
  That we one jot of former love retain.

Now at the last gasp of Love's latest breath,
  When, his pulse failing, Passion speechless lies,
When Faith is kneeling by his bed of death,
  And Innocence is closing up his eyes;

  Now, if thou would'st, when all have given him over,
    From death to life thou might'st him yet recover.

38   *Early Love*

Ah! I remember well (and how can I
But evermore remember well) when first
Our flame began, when scarce we knew what was
The flame we felt; when as we sat and sighed
And looked upon each other, and conceived
Not what we ailed – yet something we did ail;
And yet were well, and yet we were not well,
And what was our disease we could not tell.
Then would we kiss, then sigh, then look; and thus
In that first garden of our simpleness
We spent our childhood. But when years began
To reap the fruit of knowledge, ah, how then
Would she with graver looks, with sweet, stem brow,
Check my presumption and my forwardness;
    Yet still would give me flowers, still wound me, show
    What she would have me, yet not have me know.

39 *Love Is a Sickness*

Love is a sickness full of woes,
　　All remedies refusing;
A plant that most with cutting grows,
　　Most barren with best using.
　　　Why so?
More we enjoy it, more it dies,
　　If not enjoyed, it sighing cries,
　　　Heigh-ho!

Love is a torment of the mind,
　　A tempest everlasting;
And Jove hath made it of a kind
　　Not well, nor full nor fasting.
　　　Why so?
More we enjoy it, more it dies,
　　If not enjoyed, it sighing cries,
　　　Heigh-ho!

40

Look, Delia, How We Steem the Half-blown Rose

FROM *Delia*

Look, Delia, how we steem the half-blown rose,
  The image of thy blush and summer's honour;
Whilst in her tender green she doth enclose
  That pure sweet beauty Time bestows upon her.
No sooner spreads her glory in the air
  But straight her full-blown pride is in declining;
She then is scorned that late adorned the fair:
  So clouds thy beauty after fairest shining.
No April can revive thy withered flowers,
  Whose blooming grace adorns thy glory now;
Swift speedy Time, feathered with flying hours,
  Dissolves the beauty of the fairest brow.
O let not then such riches waste in vain,
  But love whilst that thou mayst be loved again.

41 *Unto the Boundless Ocean of Thy Beauty*

Unto the boundless ocean of thy beauty,
Runs this poor river, charged with streams of zeal
Returning thee the tribute of my duty,
Which here my love, my youth, my plaints reveal.
Here I unclasp the book of my charg'd soul,
Where I have cast th'accounts of all my care:
Here have I summ'd my sighs; here I enroll
How they were spent for thee; look what they are,
Look on the dear expenses of my youth,
And see how just I reckon with thine eyes:
Examine well thy beauty with my truth;
And cross my cares, ere greater sums arise.
    Read it, sweet maid, tho' it be done but slightly;
    Who can show all his love, doth love but lightly.

42 *The Passionate Shepherd to His Love*

Come live with me, and be my love,
And we will all the pleasures prove,
That valleys, groves, hills, and fields,
Woods, or steepy mountain yields.

And we will sit upon the rocks,
Seeing the shepherds feed their flocks,
By shallow rivers to whose falls
Melodious birds sing madrigals.

And I will make thee beds of roses,
And a thousand fragrant posies,
A cap of flowers, and a kirtle,
Embroidered all with leaves of myrtle;

A gown made of the finest wool,
Which from our pretty lambs we pull;
Fair lined slippers for the cold,
With buckles of the purest gold;

A belt of straw and ivy buds,
With coral clasps and amber studs:
And if these pleasures may thee move,
Come live with me, and be my love.

WILLIAM SHAKESPEARE (1564–1616)

43 *Who Is Silvia?*

FROM *The Two Gentlemen of Verona*

Who is Silvia? what is she,
    That all our swains commend her?
Holy, fair, and wise is she;
    The heaven such grace did lend her,
That she might admired be.

Is she kind as she is fair?
    For beauty lives with kindness.
Love doth to her eyes repair,
    To help him of his blindness;
And, being helped, inhabits there.

Then to Silvia let us sing,
    That Silvia is excelling;
She excels each mortal thing
    Upon the dull earth dwelling;
To her let us garlands bring.

WILLIAM SHAKESPEARE

44   *Under the Greenwood Tree*

FROM *As You Like It*

Under the greenwood tree
Who loves to lie with me,
And turn his merry note
Unto the sweet bird's throat,
Come hither, come hither, come hither!
Here shall he see
No enemy
But winter and rough weather.

Who doth ambition shun,
And loves to live i' the sun,
Seeking the food he eats,
And pleased with what he gets,
Come hither, come hither, come hither!
Here shall he see
No enemy
But winter and rough weather.

45   *It Was a Lover and His Lass*

FROM *As You Like It*

It was a lover and his lass,
  With a hey, and a ho, and a hey nonino,
That o'er the green corn-field did pass,
  In spring time, the only pretty ring time,
When birds do sing, hey ding a ding, ding;
Sweet lovers love the spring.

Between the acres of the rye,
  With a hey, and a ho, and a hey nonino,
These pretty country folks would lie,
  In spring time, the only pretty ring time,
When birds do sing, hey ding a ding, ding;
Sweet lovers love the spring.

This carol they began that hour,
　With a hey, and a ho, and a hey nonino,
How that a life was but a flower
　In spring time, the only pretty ring time,
When birds do sing, hey ding a ding, ding;
Sweet lovers love the spring.

And therefore take the present time,
　With a hey, and a ho, and a hey nonino,
For love is crowned with the prime
　In spring time, the only pretty ring time,
When birds do sing, hey ding a ding, ding;
Sweet lovers love the spring.

WILLIAM SHAKESPEARE

46 *O Mistress Mine*

<small>FROM</small> *Twelfth Night*

O mistress mine, where are you roaming?
Oh, stay and hear; your true love's coming,
   That can sing both high and low.
Trip no further, pretty sweeting;
Journeys end in lovers meeting,
   Every wise man's son doth know.

What is love? 'Tis not hereafter;
Present mirth hath present laughter;
   What's to come is still unsure.
In delay there lies no plenty;
Then come kiss me, sweet and twenty,
   Youth's a stuff will not endure.

47

Who Will Believe My Verse in Time to Come?

Who will believe my verse in time to come,
   If it were fill'd with your most high deserts?
Though yet, heaven knows, it is but as a tomb
   Which hides your life, and shows not half your parts.

If I could write the beauty of your eyes,
   And in fresh numbers number all your graces,
The age to come would say, 'This poet lies,
   Such heavenly touches ne'er touch'd earthly faces.'

So should my papers, yellow'd with their age,
   Be scorn'd, like old men of less truth than tongue;
And your true rights be term'd a poet's rage,
   And stretched metre of an antique song:

     But were some child of yours alive that time,
     You should live twice, in it and in my rime.

[SONNET 17]

48

Shall I Compare Thee to a Summer's Day?

Shall I compare thee to a summer's day?
    Thou art more lovely and more temperate:
Rough winds do shake the darling buds of May,
    And summer's lease hath all too short a date:

Sometime too hot the eye of heaven shines,
    And often is his gold complexion dimm'd:
And every fair from fair sometime declines,
    By chance, or nature's changing course untrimm'd;

But thy eternal summer shall not fade,
    Nor lose possession of that fair thou ow'st,
Nor shall death brag thou wander'st in his shade,
    When in eternal lines to time thou grow'st;

      So long as men can breathe, or eyes can see,
      So long lives this, and this gives life to thee.

[SONNET 18]

49

Nor Marble, Nor the Gilded Monuments

Nor marble, nor the gilded monuments
    Of princes, shall outlive this powerful rhyme;
But you shall shine more bright in these contents
    Than unswept stone, besmear'd with sluttish time.

When wasteful war shall statues overturn,
    And broils root out the work of masonry,
Nor Mars his sword nor war's quick fire shall burn
    The loving record of your memory.

'Gainst death and all-oblivious enmity
    Shall you pace forth; your praise still shall find room,
Even in the eyes of all posterity
    That wears this world out to the ending doom.

    So, till the judgement that yourself arise.
    You live in this, and dewll in lovers' eyes.

[SONNET 55]

50

No Longer Mourn for Me When I am Dead

No longer mourn for me when I am dead
  Than you shall hear the surly sullen bell
Give warning to the world that I am fled
  From this vile world, with vilest worm to dwell:

Nay, if you read this line, remember not
  The hand that writ it; for I love you so,
That I in your sweet thoughts would be forgot,
  If thinking on me then should make you woe.

O, if, I say, you look upon this verse
  When I perhaps compounded am with clay,
Do not so much as my poor name rehearse,
  But let your love even with my life decay,

    Lest the wise world should look into your moan
    And mock you with me after I am gone.

[SONNET 71]

51

Farewell! Thou Art too Dear for My Possessing

Farewell! thou art too dear for my possessing,
   And like enough thou knowest thy estimate:
The charter of thy worth gives thee releasing;
   My bonds in thee are all determinate.

For how do I hold thee but by thy granting?
   And for that riches where is my deserving?
The cause of this fair gift in me is wanting,
   And so my patent back again is swerving.

Thyself thou gavest, thy own worth then not knowing,
   Or me, to whom thou gavest it, else mistaking;
So thy great gift, upon misprision growing,
   Comes home again. on better judgement making.

   Thus have I had thee, as a dream doth flatter,
   In sleep a king, but walking no such matter.

[SONNET 87]

52

Let Me Not to the Marriage of True Minds

Let me not to the marriage of true minds
    Admit impediments. Love is not love
Which alters when it alteration finds,
    Or bends with the remover to remove:

O, no! it is an ever-fixed mark,
    That looks on tempests and is never shaken;
It is the star to every wandering bark,
    Whose worth's unknown, although his height be taken.

Love's not Time's fool, though rosy lips and cheeks
    Within his bending sickle's compass come;
Love alters not with his brief hours and weeks,
    But bears it out even to the edge of doom.

    If this be error, and upon me prov'd,
    I never writ, nor no man ever lov'd.

[SONNET 116]

WILLIAM SHAKESPEARE

53

My Mistress' Eyes Are Nothing Like the Sun

My mistress' eyes are nothing like the sun,
 Coral is far more red than her lips red,
If snow be white, why then her breasts are dun,
 If hairs be wires, black wires grow on her head.

I have seen roses damasked, red and white,
 But no such roses see I in her cheeks,
And in some perfumes is there more delight
 Than in the breath that from my mistress reeks.

I love to hear her speak, yet well I know
 That music hath a far more pleasin, sound,
I grant I never saw a goddess go,
 My mistress when she walks treads on the ground.

  And yet, by heaven, I think my love as rare
  As any she belied with false compare.

[SONNET 130]

54

When My Love Swears that She is Made of Truth

When my love swears that she is made of truth,
　I do believe her, though I know she lies,
That she might think me some untutor'd youth,
　Unlearned in the world's false subtleties.

Thus vainly thinking that she thinks me young,
　Although she knows my days are past the best,
Simply I credit her false-speaking tongue:
　On both sides thus is simple truth supprest.

But wherefore says she not she is unjust?
　And wherefore say not I that I am old?
O, love's best habit is in seeming trust,
　And age in love loves not to have years told:

　　Therefore I lie with her and she with me,
　　And in our faults by lies we flatter'd be.

[SONNET 138]

55

My Love Is As a Fever

My love is as a fever, longing still
  For that which longer nurseth the disease;
Feeding on that which doth preserve the ill,
  The uncertain sickly appetite to please.

My reason, the physician to my love,
  Angry that his prescriptions are not kept,
Hath left me, and I desperate now approve
  Desire is death, which physic did except.

Past cure I am, now Reason is past care,
  And frantic-mad with evermore unrest;
My thoughts and my discourse as madmen's are,
  At random from the truth vainly express'd;

  For I have sworn thee fair, and thought thee bright,
    Who art as black as hell, as dark as night.

[SONNET 147]

56   *Thou Art Not Fair*

Thou art not fair, for all thy red and white,
For all those rosy ornaments in thee;
Thou art not sweet, though made of mere delight,
Not fair nor sweet, unless thou pity me.
I will not soothe thy fanc'es: thou shalt prove
That beauty is no beauty without love.

Yet love not me, nor seek thou to allure
My thoughts with beauty, were it more divine:
Thy smiles and kisses I cannot endure,
I'll not be wrapped up in those arms of thine:
Now show it, if thou be a woman right –
Embrace, and kiss, and love me, in despite!

SIR WILLIAM ALEXANDER,
EARL OF STIRLING (1567–1640)

57   I'll Give Thee Leave, My Love

I'll give thee leave, my love, in beauty's field
To rear red colours whiles, and bend thine eyes;
Those that are bashful still, I quite despise
Such simple souls are too soon moved to yield:
Let majesty armed in thy countenance sit,
As that which will no injury receive;
And I'll not hate thee, whiles although thou have
A spark of pride, so it be ruled by wit.
This is to chastity a powerful guard,
Whilst haughty thoughts all servile things eschew,
That spark hath power the passions to subdue,
And would of glory challenge a reward:
    But do not fall in love with thine own self;
    Narcissus erst was lost on such a shelf.

SIR HENRY WOTTON (1568–1639)

58   A Youthful Poem

O faithless world, and thy most faithless part,
   A woman's heart!
The true shop of variety, where sits
   Nothing but fits
And fevers of desire, and pangs of love,
   Which toys remove.
Why was she born to please? or I to trust
   Words writ in dust,
Suffering her eyes to govern my despair,
   My pain for air;
And fruit of time rewarded with untruth,
   The food of youth?
Untrue she was; yet I believed her eyes,
   Instructed spies,
I was taught, that love was but a school
   To breed a fool.

Or sought she more, by triumphs of denial,
    To make a trial
How far her smiles commanded my weakness?
    Yield, and confess!
Excuse no more thy folly; but, for cure,
    Blush and endure
As well thy shame as passions that were vain;
    And think, 'tis gain,
To know that love lodged in a woman's breast
    Is but a guest.

59 *My Love and I Must Part*

Weep eyes, break heart
My love and I must part.
Cruel fates true love do soonest sever;
O, I shall see thee never, never, never!
O, happy is the maid whose life takes end
Ere it knows parent's frown or loss of friend!
Weep eyes, break heart!
My love and I must part.

60   *Begging Another*

For love's sake, kiss me once again!
I long, and should not beg in vain.
Here's none to spy or see;
Why do you doubt or stay?
I'll taste as lightly as the bee,
That doth but touch his flower, and flies away.

Once more, and faith, I will be gone –
Can he that loves ask less than one?
Nay, you may err in this,
And all your bounty wrong:
This could be called but half a kiss;
What we're but once to do, we should do long.

I will but mend the last, and tell
Where, how, it would have relished well;
Join lip to lip, and try:
Each suck the other's breath,
And whilst our tongues perplexèd lie,
Let who will think us dead, or wish our death!

61 *Love's Sickness*

Wretched and foolish jealousy
How cam'st thou thus to enter me?
   I ne'er was of thy kind:
Nor have I yet the narrow mind
   To vent that poor desire,
That others should not warm them at my fire:
   I wish the sun should shine
On all men's fruits and flowers as well as mine.

But under the disguise of love,
Thou say'st thou only cam'st to prove
   What my affections were.
Think'st thou that love is helped by fear?
   Go, get thee quickly forth,
Love's sickness and his noted want of worth,
   Seek doubting men to please.
I ne'er will owe my health to a disease.

62 *Song to Celia*

Drink to me only with thine eyes,
And I will pledge with mine;
Or leave a kiss but in the cup
And I'll not look for wine.
The thirst that from thy soul doth rise
Doth ask a drink divine:
But might I of Jove's nectar sup,
I would not change for thine.

I sent thee late a rosy wreath,
Not so much honouring thee
As giving it a hope that there
It could not withered be.
But thou thereon did'st only breathe,
And send'st it back to me:
Since when it grows, and smells, I swear,
Not of itself, but thee.

63 *Still to Be Neat, Still to Be Drest*

Still to be neat, still to be drest,
As you were going to a feast;
Still to be powder'd, still perfumed:
Lady, it's to be presumed,
That arts' hid causes are not found,
All is not sweet, all is not sound.
Give me a look, give me a face,
That makes simplicity a grace;
Robes loosely flowing, hair as free:
Such sweet neglect more taketh me,
Than all th' adulteries of art,
They strike mine eyes, but not my heart.

64   *Golden Fetters*

Whilst I behold thy glittering golden hairs
Dishevelled thus, waving about thy ears,
And see those locks thus loosèd and undone
For their more pomp to sport them in the sun,
Love takes those threads and weaves them with that art
He knits a thousand knots about my heart
And with such skill and cunning he them sets,
My soul lies taken in those lovely nets,
Making me cry, 'Fair prison, that dost hold
My heart in letters wrought of burnished gold.'

65 *The Good-morrow*

I wonder by my troth, what thou and I
Did, till we loved? were we not weaned till then?
But sucked on country pleasures, childishly?
Or snorted we in the seven sleepers' den?
'Twas so; but this, all pleasures' fancies be.
If ever any beauty I did see,
Which I desired, and got, 'twas but a dream of thee.

And now good-morrow to our waking souls,
Which watch not one another out of fear;
For love all love of other sights controls,
And makes one little room an everywhere.
Let sea-discoverers to new worlds have gone,
Let maps to other, worlds on worlds have shown,
Let us possess one world, each hath one, and is one.

My face in thine eye, thine in mine appears,
And true plain hearts do in the faces rest;
Where can we find two better hemispheres
Without sharp North, without declining West?
What ever dies, was not mixed equally;
If our two loves be one, or thou and I
Love so alike that none do slacken, none can die.

66   *A Lecture upon the Shadow*

Stand still, and I will read to thee
A lecture, love, in love's philosophy.
    These three hours that we have spent,
    Walking here, two shadows went
Along with its, which we ourselves produced;
But, now the sun is just above our head,
    We do those shadows tread;
    And to brave clearness all things are reduced.
  So whilst our infant loves did grow,
  Disguises did, and shadows, flow,
  From us, and our care; but, now 'tis not so.

That love hath not attained the high'st degree,
Which is still diligent lest others see.

Except our loves at this noon stirs
shall new shadows make the other was. ,
    As the first were made to blind
    Others; these which come behind
Will work upon ourselves, and blind our eyes.
If our loves faint, and westwardly decline;
    To me thou, falsely, thine,
    And I to thee mine actions shall disguise.
  The morning shadows wear away,
  But these grow longer all the day,
  But oh, love's day, is short, if love decay.

Love is a growing, or full constant light;
And his first minute, after noon, is night.

67   *Love's Growth*

I scarce believe my love to be so pure
   As I had thought it was,
   Because it doth endure
Vicissitude, and season, as the grass;
Methinks I lied all winter, when I swore
My love was infinite, if spring make it more.

But if this medicine, love, which cures all sorrow
   With more, not only be no quintessence,
   But mix'd of all stuffs, vexing soul, or sense,
And of the sun lets active vigour borrow,
Love's not so pure, and abstract, as they use
To say, which have no mistress but their Muse;
But as all else, being elemented too,
Love sometimes would contemplate, sometimes do.

And yet no greater, but more eminent,
    Love by the spring is grown;
    As in the firmament
Stars by the sun are not enlarged, but shown,
Gentle love deeds, as blossoms on a bough,
From love's awaken'd root do bud out now.

If, as in water stirr'd more circles be
    Produced by one, love such additions take,
    Those like so many spheres but one heaven make,
For they are all concentric unto thee;
And though each spring do add to love new heat,
As princes do in times of action get
New taxes, and remit them not in peace,
No winter shall abate this spring's increase.

68 *Love's Infiniteness*

If yet I have not all thy love,
Dear, I shall never have it all
I cannot breathe one other sigh, to move,
Nor can entreat one other tear to tall,
And all my treasure, which should purchase thee,
Sighs, tears, and oaths, and letters I have spent.
Yet no more can be due to me,
Than at the bargain made was meant,
If then thy gift of love were partial,
That some to me, some should to others fall,
   Dear, I shall never have thee all.

Or if then thou gavest me all,
All was but all, which thou hadst then;
But if in thy heart, since, there be or shall,
New love created be, by other men,

Which have their stocks entire. and can in tears,
In sighs, in oaths, and letter outbid me.
This new love may begot new fears,
For, this love was not vowed by thee,
And yet it was, thy gift being general,
The ground, thy heart is mine, what ever shall
   Grow there, dear, I should have it all.

Yet I would not have all yet,
He that hath all can have no more,
And since my love doth every day admit
New growth, thou shouldst have new rewards in stoic;
Thou canst not every day give me thy heart,
If thou canst give it, then thou never gayest it:
Love's riddles are, that though thy heart depart,
It stays at home, and thou with losing savest it:
But we will have a way more liberal,
Than changing hearts, to join them, so we shall
   Be one, and one another's all.

69   *The Expiration*

So, so, break off this last lamenting kiss,
    Which sucks two souls, and vapours both away,
Turn thou ghost that way, and let me turn this,
    And let our selves benight our happiest day,
We asked none leave to love; nor will we owe
    Any so cheap a death as saying, Go;

Go; and if that word have not quite killed thee,
    Ease me with death, by bidding me go too.
Oh, if it have, let my word work on me,
    And a just office on a murderer do.
Except it be too late, to kill me so,
    Being double dead, going, and bidding, go.

70   *Golden Slumbers*

Golden slumbers kiss your eyes,
Smiles awake you when you rise:
Sleep, pretty wantons, do not cry,
And I will sing a lullaby.
Rock them, rock them, lullaby.

Care is heavy, therefore sleep you.
You are care, and care must keep you:
Sleep, pretty wantons, do not cry,
And I will sing a lullaby.
Rock them, rock them, lullaby.

THOMAS DEKKER

71   *O the Month of May*

FROM *The Shoemaker's Holiday*

O the month of May, the merry month of May,
  So frolic, so gay, and so green, so green, so green!
O and then did I unto my true love say,
  Sweet Peg, thou shalt be my Summer's Queen.

Now the nightingale, the pretty nightingale,
  The sweetest singer in all the forest's choir,
Entreats thee, sweet Peggy, to hear thy true love's tale:
  Lo, yonder she sitteth, her breast against a briar.

But O I spy the cuckoo, the cuckoo, the cuckoo;
  See where she sitteth; come away, my joy:
Come away, I prithee, I do not like the cuckoo
  Should sing where my Peggy and I kiss and toy.

O the month of May, the merry month of May,
　　So frolic, so gay, and so green, so green, so green!
And then did I unto my true love say,
　　Sweet Peg, thou shalt be my Summer's Queen.

72   *A Portrait*

My Infelice's face, her brow, her eye,
The dimple on her cheek; and such sweet skill
Hath from the cunning workman's pencil flown,
These lips look fresh and lovely as her own.
False colours last after the true be dead.
Of all the roses grafted on her cheeks,
Of all the graces dancing in her eyes,
Of all the music set upon her tongue,
Of all that was past woman's excellence
In her white bosom; look, a painted board
Circumscribes all.

73   *A Sonnet of the Moon*

Look how the pale queen of the silent night
  Doth cause the ocean to attend upon her,
And he, as long as she is in his sight,
  With his full tide is ready her to honour:

But when the silver wagon of the moon
  Is mounted up so high he cannot follow,
The sea calls home his crystal waves to moan,
  And with low ebb doth manifest his sorrow.

So you, that are the sovereign of my heart,
  Have all my joys attending on your will:
My joys low ebbing when you do depart,
  When you return, their tide my heart doth fill.

    So as you come, and as you do depart,
    Joys ebb and flow within my tender heart.

74 *Bereavement*

What doth it serve to see sun's burning face?
And skies enamelled with both Indies' gold?
Or moon at night in jettie chariot rolled?
And all the glory of that starry place?
What doth it serve earth's beauty to behold?
The mountain's pride, the meadow's flowery grace;
The stately comeliness of forests old,
The sport of clouds which would themselves embrace?
What doth it serve to heare the sylvan songs
The wanton mearle,* the nightingale's sad strains,
Which in dark shades seem to deplore my wrongs?
For what doth serve all that this world contains,
    Since she for whom those once to me were dear
    No part of them can have now with me here.

* blackbird

LADY MARY WROTH (1586–1640)

75 *Cupid Lost*

Late in the forest I did Cupid see
  Cold, wet, and crying he had lost his way,
  And being blind was farther like to stray:
Which sight a kind compassion bred in me,

I kindly took, and dried him, while that he
  Poor child complained he starvèd was with stay,
  And pined for want of his accustomed play,
For none in that wild place his host would be,

I glad was of his finding, thinking sure
  This service should my freedom still procure,
    And in my arms I took him then unharmed,

Carrying him safe unto a myrtle bower
  But in the way he made me feel his power,
    Burning my heart who had him kindly warmed.

76   *Love, a Child, Is Ever Crying*

Love, a child, is ever crying;
Please him, and he straight is flying;
Give him, he the more is craving.
Never satisfied with having.

His desires have no measure;
Endless folly is his treasure;
What he promiseth he breaketh;
Trust not one word that he speaketh.

He vows nothing but false matter;
And to cozen you will flatter;
Let him gain the hand, he'll leave you,
And still glory to deceive you.

He will triumph in your wailing;
And yet cause be of your failing:
These his virtues are, and slighter
Are his gifts, his favours lighter.

Fathers are as firm in staying;
Wolves no fiercer in their preying:
As a child, then, leave him crying;
Nor seek him so given to flying.

77   *Cherry Ripe, Ripe, I Cry*

Cherry ripe, ripe, I cry,
Full and fair ones; come and buy:
If so be, you ask me where
They do grow? I answer, 'There,
Where my Julia's lips do smile
There's the land, or Cherry Isle:
Whose plantations fully show
All the year, where Cherries grow.'

78 *Chop-cherry*

Thou gav'st me leave to kiss,
  Thou gav'st me leave to woo;
Thou mad'st me think, by this
  And that, thou lov'st me too.

But I shall ne'er forget
  How, for to make thee merry
Thou mad'st me chop, but yet
  Another snapped the cherry.

79   *Delight in Disorder*

A sweet disorder in the dress
Kindles in clothes a wantonness:
A lawn about the shoulders thrown
Into a fine distraction,
An erring lace, which here and there
Enthrals the crimson stomacher,
A cuff neglectful and thereby
Ribbands to flow confusedly,
A winning wave, deserving note,
In the tempestuous petticoat,
A careless shoestring, in whose tie
I see a wild civility,
Do more bewitch me, than when art
Is too precise in every part.

80   *I Abhor the Slimy Kiss*

I abhor the slimy kiss,
(which to me most loathsome is).
Those lips please me which are placed
Close, but not too strictly laced.
Yielding I would have them; yet
Not a wimbling tongue admit:
What should poking-sticks make there,
When the ruff is set elsewhere ?

81   *The Night-Piece, to Julia*

Her eyes the glow-worm lend thee,
The shooting stars attend thee;
   And the elves also,
   Whose little eyes glow
Like the sparks of fire, befriend thee.

No will-o'-the-wisp mislight thee;
Nor snake or slow-worm bite thee;
   But on, on thy way
   Not making a stay,
Since ghost there's none to affright thee.

Let not the dark thee cumber.
What though the moon does slumber?
   The stars of the night
   Will lend thee their light,
Like tapers clear without number.

Then, Julia, let me woo thee,
Thus, thus to come unto me;
    And when I shall meet
    Thy silvery feet,
My soul I'll pour into thee.

82 *No Loathsomeness in Love*

What I fancy, I approve,
No dislike there is in love:
Be my mistress short or tall,
And distorted therewithal:
Be she likewise one of those,
That an acre hath of nose:
Be her forehead, and her eyes
Full of incongruities:
Be her cheeks so shallow too,
As to shew her tongue wag through:
Be her lips ill hung, or set,
And her grinders black as jet;
Has she thin hair, hath she none,
She's to me a paragon.

83   *Of Love*

How love came in, I do not know,
Whether by th'eye, or ear, or no:
Or whether with the soul it came
(At first) infused with the same:
Whether in part 'tis here or there,
Or, like the soul, whole everywhere:
This troubles me: but I as well
As any other, this can tell;
That when from hence she does depart,
The out-let then is from the heart.

84 *The Shepherd to His Fair One*

Live, live with me, and thou shalt see
The pleasures I'll prepare for thee.
The soft sweet moss shall be thy bed,
With crawling woodbine overspread,
By which the silver-shedding streams
Shall gently melt thee into dreams.
Thy clothing neat shall be a gown
Made of the fleece's purest down.
The tongues of kids shall be thy meat,
Their milk thy drink, and thou shalt eat
The paste of filberts for thy bread,
With cream of cowslips butterbd.
Thy feasting tables shall be hills,
With daisies spread and daffodils,
Where thou shalt sit, and redbreast by
For meat shall give thee melody.

I'll give thee chains and carcanets
Of primroses and violets.
These – nay, and more – thine own shall
If thou wilt love and live with me.

85 *To Anthea*

Ah my Anthea! Must my heart still break?
(Love makes me write, what shame forbids to speak.)
Give me a kiss, and to that kiss a score;
Then to that twenty, add an hundred more:
A thousand to that hundred: so kiss on,
To make that thousand up a million.
Treble that million, and when that is done,
Let's kiss afresh, as when we first begun.
But yet, though love likes well such scenes as these,
There is an act that will more fully please:
Kissing and glancing, soothing, all make way
But to the acting of this private play:
Name it I would; but being blushing red,
The rest I'll speak, when we meet both in bed.

86

To Anthea, who May Command Him Anything

Bid me to live, and I will live
    Thy Protestant to be;
Or bid me love, and I will give
    A loving heart to thee.

A heart as soft, a heart as kind,
    A heart as sound and free,
As in the whole world thou can'st find,
    That heart I'll give to thee.

Bid that heart stay, and it will stay,
    To honour thy decree;
Or bid it languish quite away,
    And 't shall do so for thee.

Bid me to weep, and I will weep,
   While I have eyes to see;
And having none, yet I will keep
   A heart to weep for thee.

Bid me despair, and I'll despair,
   Under that cypress-tree;
Or bid me die, and I will dare
   E'en death, to die for thee

Thou art my life, my love, my heart
   The very eyes of me;
And hast command of every part,
   To live and die for thee.

87 *To Electra*

I dare not ask a kiss;
   I dare not beg a smile;
Lest having that, or this,
   I might grow proud the while.

No, no, the utmost share
   Of my desire shall be
Only to kiss that air
   That lately kissèd thee.

ROBERT HERRICK

88   *Upon Julia's Clothes*

Whenas in silks my Julia goes,
Then, then, methinks, how sweetly flows
That liquefaction of her clothes!

Next, when I cast mine eyes and see
That brave vibration each way free,
Oh, how that glittering taketh me!

ROBERT HERRICK

89   *Upon Love*

Love scorched my finger, but did spare
  The burning of my heart:
To signify, in love my share
  Should be a little part.

Little I love; but if that he
  Would but that heat recall:
That joint to ashes burnt should be,
  Ere I would love at all.

90   *The Vine*

I dreamed this mortal part of mine
Was metamorphosed to a vine;
Which crawling one and every way,
Enthralled my dainty Lucia.
Me thought, her long small legs and thighs
I with my tendrils did surprise;
Her belly, buttocks, and her waist
By now soft nerveless were embraced:

About her head I writhing hung,
And with rich clusters (hid among
The leaves) her temples I behung
So that my Lucia seemed to me
Young Bacchus ravished by his tree.
My curls about her neck did crawl,
And arms and hands they did enthral;

So that she could not freely stir,
(All parts there made one prisoner).
But when I crept with leaves to hide
Those parts, which maids keep unespied,
Such fleeting pleasures there I took,
That with the fancy I awoke;
And found (Ah me!) this flesh of mine
More like a stock, than like a vine.

91 *The Vision to Electra*

I dreamed we both were in a bed
Of roses, almost smothered:
The warmth and sweetness had me there
Made lovingly familiar:
But that I heard thy sweet breath say,
Faults done by night, will blush by day:
I kissed thee (panting) and I call
Night to the records that was all.
But ah! if empty dreams so please,
Love give me more such nights as these.

92   *A Divine Rapture*

E'en like two little bank-dividing brooks,
　　That wash the pebbles with their wanton streams,
And having ranged and searched a thousand nooks,
　　Meet both at length in silver-breasted Thames,
　　　　Where in a greater current they conjoin:
　　　　So I my best-belovèd's am; so is mine.

E'en so we met; and after long pursuit,
　　E'en so we joined; we both became entire;
No need for either to renew a suit,
　　For I was flax and he was flames of fire:
　　　　Our firm-united souls did more than mine;
　　　　So I my best-belovèd's am; so he is mine.

It all those glittering monarchs that command
    The servile quarters of this earthly ball,
Should tender in exchange, their shares of land,
    I would not change my fortunes for them all.
        Their wealth is but a counter to my coin:
        The world's but theirs; but my belovèd's mine.

93 Love's Matrimony

There is no happy life
But in a wife;
The comforts are so sweet
When they do meet:
'Tis plenty, peace, a calm
Like dropping balm:
Love's weather is so fair,
Perfumèd air,
Each word such pleasure brings
Like soft-touched strings;
Love's passion moves the heart
On either part.
Such harmony together,
So pleased in either,

No discords, concords still,
Sealed with one will.
By love, God man made one,
Yet not alone:
Like stamps of king and queen
It may be seen,
Two figures but one coin;
So they do join,
Only they not embrace,
We face to face.

94 *Love*

Love bade me welcome; yet my soul drew back,
      Guilty of dust and sin
But quick-eyed love, observing me grow slack
      From my first entrance in,
Drew nearer to me, sweetly questioning,
      If I lacked anything.

'A guest,' I answered, 'worthy to be here.'
      Love said, 'You shall be he.'
'I, the unkind, ungrateful? Ah, my dear.
      I cannot look on thee.'
Love took my hand, and smiling did reply,
      'Who made the eyes but I?'

'Truth, Lord, but I have marred them; let my shame
        Go where it doth deserve.'
'And I know you not,' says Love, 'who bore the blame?'
                'My dear, then I will serve.'
'You must sit down,' says Love, 'and taste my meat.'
                So I did sit and eat.

THOMAS CAREW (1595–1640)

95 *He that Loves a Rosy Cheek*

He that loves a rosy cheek,
  Or a coral lip admires,
Or from star-like eyes doth seek
  Fuel to maintain his fires;
    As old Time makes these decay,
    So his flames must waste away.

But a smooth and steadfast mind,
  Gentle thoughts and calm desires,
Hearts with equal love combined,
  Kindle never-dying fires;
    Where these are not, I despise
    Lovely cheeks, or lips, or eyes.

96   *To My Inconstant Mistress*

When thou, poor excommunicate
 From all the joys of love, shalt see
The full reward, and glorious fate,
 Which my strong faith shall purchase me,
Then curse thine own inconstancy.

A fairer hand than thine, shall cure
 That heart, which thy false oaths did wound;
And to my soul, a soul more pure
 Than thine, shall by love's hand be bound,
And both with equal glory crowned.

Then shalt thou weep, entreat, complain
 To love, as I did once to thee;
When all thy tears shall be as vain
 As mine were then, for thou shalt be
Damned for thy false apostasy.

97   *Youth and Beauty*

Thou art so fair, and young withal,
    Thou kindl'st young desires in me,
Restoring life to leaves that fall,
    And sight to eyes that hardly see
    Half those fresh beauties bloom in thee.

Those, under sev'ral herbs and flow'rs
    Disguised, were all Medea gave,
When she recalled time's flying hours,
    And aged Aeson from his grave,
    For beauty can both kill and save.

Youth it enflames, but age it cheers,
    I would go back, but not return
To twenty but to twice those years;
    Not blaze, but ever constant bum,
    For fear my cradle prove my urn.

98   *Chloris in the Snow*

I saw fair Chloris walk alone,
   Whilst feathered rain came softly down,
And Jove descended from his tower
   To court her in a silver shower.
The wanton snow flew on her breast
   Like little birds unto their nest;
But overcome with whiteness there,
   For grief it thawed into a tear;
Thence, falling on her garment's hem,
   To deck her, froze into a gem.

99   *Phyllis*

Poor credulous and simple maid!
By what strange wiles art thou betrayed!
  A treasure thou has lost today
  For which thou can'st no ransom pay.
How black art thou transformed with sin!
How strange a guilt gnaws me within!
  Grief will convert this red to pale;
  When every wake, and witsund-ale
Shall talk my shame; break, break sad heart
There is no medecine for my smart,
  No herb nor balm can cure my sorrow,
  Unless you meet again tomorrow.

100 *Under the Willow-shades*

Under the willow-shades they were
   Free from the eye-sight of the sun,
For no intruding beam could there
   Peep through to spy what things were done:
     Thus sheltered they unseen did lie,
     Surfeiting on each other's eye;
Defended by the willow-shades alone,
The sun's heat they defied and cooled their own.

Whilst they did embrace unspied,
   The conscious willow seemed to smile,
That them with privacy supplied,
   Holding the door, as 't were, the while;
     And when their dalliances were o'er,
     The willows, to oblige them more,
Bowing, did seem to say, as they withdrew,
'We can supply you with a cradle too.'

101　To Amoret

Amoret! The Milky Way
　　Framed of many nameless stars!
The smooth stream where none can say
　　He this drop to that prefers!

Amoret! My lovely foe!
　　Tell me where thy strength does lie?
Where the power that charms us so?
　　In thy soul, or in thy eye?

By that snowy neck alone,
　　Or thy grace in motion seen,
No such wonders could be done;
　　Yet thy waist is straight and clean
As Cupid's shaft, or Hermes' rod,
　　And powerful, too, as either god.

102   To a Very Young Lady

Lucy Sidney

Why came I so untimely forth
Into a world which, wanting thee,
Could entertain us with no worth
Or shadow of felicity,
That time should me so far remove
From that which I was born to love?

Yet, fairest blossom! do not slight
That age which may know so soon;
The rosy morn resigns her light,
And milder glory, to the noon;
And then what wonders shall you do,
Whose dawning beauty warms us so?

Hope waits upon the flowery prime;
And summer, though it be less gay,
Yet is not looked on as a time
Of declination or decay;
For with a full hand that does bring
All that was promised by the spring.

103   *To Flavia*

'Tis not your beauty can engage
My wary heart;
The sun, in all his pride and rage,
Has not that art;
And yet he shines as bright as you,
If brightness could our souls subdue.

'Tis not the pretty things you say,
Nor those you write,
Which can make Thyrsis' heart your prey;
For that delight,
The graces of a well-taught mind,
In some of our own sex we find.

No, Flavia! 'Tis your love I fear;
Love's surest darts,
Those which so seldom fail him, are
Headed with hearts;
Their very shadows make us yield;
Dissemble well, and win the field.

104 *While I Listen to Thy Voice*

While I listen to thy voice,
Chloris! I feel my life decay;
That powerful noise
Calls my flitting soul away.
Oh! suppress that magic sound,
Which destroys without a wound.

Peace, Chloris! Peace! Or singing die,
That together you and I
To heaven may go;
For all we know
Of what the blessed do above,
Is, that they sing, and that they love.

105 The Bride

The maid (and thereby hangs a tale),
For such a maid no Whitson-ale
 Could ever yet produce;
No grape that's kindly ripe could be
So round so plump, so soft as she,
 Nor half so full of juice.

Her feet beneath her petticoat,
Like little mice, stole in and out,
 As if they feared the light;
But, oh! She dances such a way!
No nun upon the Easter-day
 Is half so fine in sight.

Her cheeks so rare a white was on,
   No daisy makes comparison
      (Who sees them is undone);
For streaks of red were mingled there,
Such as are on a Catherine's pear
      (The side that's next the sun).

Her lips were red; and one was thin,
Compared to that was next her chin
      (Some bee had stung it newly).
But see – her eyes so guard her face,
I durst no more upon them gaze
      Than on the sun in July.

Her mouth so small, when she does speak,
Thou'dst swear her teeth her words did break,
      That they might passage get;
But she so handled still the matter,
They came as good as ours, or better,
      And are not spent a whit.

SIR JOHN SUCKLING

106   *Out Upon It*

Out upon it, I have loved
    Three whole days together!
And am like to love three more,
    If it hold fair weather.

Time shall moult away his wings
    Ere he shall discover
In the whole wide world again
    Such a constant lover.

But a pox upon't, no praise
    There is due at all to me:
Love with me had made no stay,
    Had it any been but she.

Had it any been but she,
    And that very very face,
There had been at least ere this
    A dozen dozen in her place.

107   *Why So Pale?*

Why so pale and wan, fond lover?
   Prithee, why so pale?
Will, when looking well can't move her,
   Looking ill prevail?
   Prithee, why so pale?

Why so dull and mute, young sinner?
   Prithee, why so mute?
Will, when speaking well can't win her,
   Saying nothing do 't?
   Prithee, why so mute?

Quit, quit for shame! This will not move;
   This cannot take her.
If of herself she will not love,
   Nothing can make her:
   The devil take her!

108   *To My Dear and Loving Husband*

If ever two were one, then surely we.
If ever man were loved by wife, then thee;
If ever wife was happy in a man,
Compare with me, ye women, if you can.
I prize thy love more than whole mines of gold
Or all the riches that the East cloth hold.
My love is such that rivers cannot quench,
Nor ought but love from thee, give recompense.
Thy love is such I can no way repay,
The heavens reward thee manifold, I pray.
Then while we live, in love let's so persevere
That when we live no more, we may live ever.

109   *An Epitaph upon a Husband and Wife Buried Together*

To these whom death again did wed
This grave's the second marriage-bed.
  For though the hand of fate could force
  'Twixt soul and body a divorce,
It could not sever man and wife,
Because they both lived but one life.
  Peace, good reader, do not weep;
  Peace, the lovers are asleep.
They, sweet turtles, folded lie
In the last knot that love could tie.
  Let them sleep, let them sleep on,
  Till the stormy night be gone,
And the eternal morrow dawn;
Then the curtains will be drawn,
  And they wake into a light
  Whose day shall never die in night.

110   *To Althea, from Prison*

When Love with unconfinèd wings
   Hovers within my gates,
And my divine Althea brings
   To whisper at the grates;
When I lie tangled in her hair
   And fettered to her eye,
The birds that wanton in the air
   Know no such liberty.

When flowing cups run swiftly round
   With no allaying Thames,
Our careless heads with roses crowned,
   Our hearts with loyal flames;
When thirsty grief in wine we steep,
   When healths and draughts go free,
Fishes that tipple in the deep
   Know no such liberty.

When, linnet-like confinèd, I
    With shriller throat shall sing
The sweetness, mercy, majesty
    And glories of my King;
When I shall voice aloud how good
    He is, how great should be,
Enlargèd winds that curl the flood
    Know no such liberty.

Stone walls do not a prison make,
    Nor iron bars a cage;
Minds innocent and quiet take
    That for an hermitage:
If I have freedom in my love
    And in my soul am free,
Angels alone that soar above
    Enjoy such liberty.

111 *To Lucasta, Going Beyond the Wars*

Tell me not, sweet, I am unkind,
  That from the nunnery
Of thy chaste breast and quiet mind
  To war and arms I fly.

True, a new mistress now I chase,
  The first foe in the field;
And with a stronger faith embrace
  A sword, a horse, a shield.

Yet this inconstancy is such
  As you too shall adore;
I could not love thee, dear, so much,
  Loved I not honour more.

112   *Why Do I Love Her?*

'Tis not her birth, her friends, nor yet her treasure,
Nor do I covet her for sensual pleasure,
Nor for that old morality
Do I love her, 'cause she loves me.
Sure he that loves his lady 'cause she's fair,
Delights his eye, so loves himself, not her.
Something there is moves me to love, and I
Do know I love, but know not how, nor why.

113   *The Definition of Love*

1

My love is of a birth as rare
As 'tis for object strange and high:
It was begotten by Despair
Upon Impossibility.

2

Magnanimous Despair alone
Could show me so divine a thing,
Where feeble Hope could ne'er have flown
But vainly flapped its tinsel wing.

3

And yet I quickly might arrive
Where my extended soul is fixed,
But Fate does iron wedges drive,
And always crowds itself betwixt.

4

For Fate with jealous eye does see
Two perfect loves, nor lets them close:
Their union would her ruin be,
And her tyrannic power depose.

5

And therefore her decrees of steel
Us as the distant poles have placed,
(Though Love's whole world on us doth wheel)
Not by themselves to be embraced,

6

Unless the giddy heaven fall,
And earth some new convulsion tear;
And, us to join, the world should all
Be cramped into a planisphere.

7

As lines (so loves) oblique may well
Themselves in every angle greet:
But ours so truly parallel,
Though infinite, can never meet.

8

Therefore the love which us doth bind,
But Fate so enviously debars,
Is the conjunction of the mind,
And opposition of the stars.

114 *To His Coy Mistress*

Had we but world enough, and time,
This coyness, Lady, were no crime,
We would sit down and think which way
To walk and pass our long love's day.
Thou by the Indian Ganges' side
Shouldst rubies find; I by the tide
Of Humber would complain. I would
Love you ten years before the Flood,
And you should, if you please, refuse
Till the conversion of the Jews.
My vegetable love should grow
Vaster than empires, and more slow;
An hundred years should go to praise
Thine eyes, and on thy forehead gaze,
Two hundred to adore each breast,
But thirty thousand to the rest;

An age at least to every part,
And the last age should show your heart.
For, Lady, you deserve this state,
Nor would I love at lower rate.

But at my back I always hear
Time's wingèd chariot hurrying near;
And yonder all before us lie
Deserts of vast eternity.
Thy beauty shall no more he found,
Nor, in thy marble vault shall sound
My echoing song; then worms shall try
That long preserved virginity,
And your quaint honour turn to dust,
And into ashes all my lust:
The grave s a fine and private place,
But none, I think, do there embrace.

Now therefore, while the youthful hue
Sits on thy skin like morning dew,
And while thy willing soul transpires

At every pore with instant fires,
Now let us sport us while we may,
And now, like amorous birds of prey,
Rather at once our time devour
Than languish in his slow-chapt power.
Let us roll all our strength and all
Our sweetness up into one ball,
And tear our pleasures with rough strife
Through the iron gates of life.
Thus, though we cannot make our sun
Stand still, yet we will make him run.

115   Love and Poetry

O love, how thou art tired out with rhyme!
Thou art a tree whereon all poets clime;
And from thy branches every one takes some
Of thy sweet fruit, which Fancy feeds upon.
But now thy tree is left so bare and poor,
That they can scarcely gather one plumb more.

116   *When I Lie Burning*

When I lie burning in thy eye,
   Or freezing in thy breast,
What martyrs, in wished flames that die,
   Are half so pleased or blest?

When thy soft accents, through mine ear,
   Into my soul do fly,
What angel would not quit his sphere
   To hear such harmony?

Or when the kiss thou gav'st me last
   My soul stole, in its breath,
What life would sooner be embraced
   Than so desired a death?

Then think not freedom I desire,
    Or would my fetters leave,
Since, Phoenix-like, I from this fire
    Both life and youth receive.

KATHERINE PHILIPS (1631–1664)

117 An Answer to Another Persuading a Lady to Marriage

Forbear, bold youth, all's Heaven here,
    And what you do aver,
To others, courtship may appear,
    'Tis sacriledge to her.

She is a publick deity,
    And were't not very odd
She should depose her self to be
    A petty household god?

First make the sun in private shine,
    And bid the world adieu,
That so he may his beams confine
    In complement to you.

But if of that you do despair,
   Think how you did amiss,
To strive to fix her beams which are
   More bright and large than this.

118

To My Excellent Lucasia, on Our Friendship

I did not live until this time
   Crown'd my felicity,
When I could say without a crime,
   I am not thine, but thee

This carcass breath'd, and walkt, and slept
   So that the world believ'd
There was a soul the motions kept;
   But they were all deceiv'd.

For as a watch by art is wound
   To motion, such was mine:
But never had Orinda found
   A soul till she found thine;

Which now inspires, cures and supplies,
 And guides my darkened breast:
For thou art all that I can prize,
 My joy, my life, my rest.

No bridegroom's nor crown-conqueror's mirth
 To mine compar'd can be:
They have but pieces of the earth,
 I've all the world in thee.

Then let our flames still light and shine,
 And no false fear controul,
As innocent as our design,
 Immortal as our soul.

119   *To a Lady Asking How Long*
        He Would Love Her

It is not, Celia, in our power
    To say how long our love will last;
It may be we within this hour
    May lose those joys we now do taste;
The blessèd, that immortal be,
From change in love are only free.

Then since we mortal lovers are,
    Ask not how long our love will last;
But while it does, let us take tare
    Each minute be with pleasure past:
Were it not madness to deny
To live because we're sure to die?

120   To a Very Young Lady

Sweetest bud of beauty, may
No untimely frost decay
   The early glories, which we trace
   Blooming in thy matchless face;
But kindly opening, like the rose,
Fresh beauties every day disclose,
   Such as by nature are not shown
   In all the blossoms she has blown:
And then, what conquest shall you make,
Who hearts already daily take
   Scorched in the morning with thy beams,
   How shall we bear those sad extremes
Which must attend thy threatening eyes
When thou shalt to thy noon arise?

121　*The Slight*

I did but crave that I might kiss,
　　If not her lip, at least her hand,
The coolest lover's frequent bliss;
　　And rude is she that will withstand
　　That inoffensive liberty:
She (would you think it?) in a fume
Turned her about and left the room;
　　Not she, she vowed, not she.

'Well, Clarissa,' then said I,
　　'If it must thus for ever be,
I can renounce my slavery
　　And, since you will not, can be free.'
　　Many a time she made me die,
Yet (would you think't) I loved the more;
But I'll not take't as heretofore,
　　Not I, I'll vow, not I.

122   *Celia*

Not, Celia, that I juster am
   Or better than the rest;
For I would change each hour like them,
   Were not my heart at rest.

But I am tied to very thee
   By every thought I have:
Thy face I only care to see,
   Thy heart I only crave.

All that in woman is adored,
   In thy dear self I find,
For the whole sex can but afford
   The handsome and the kind.

Why then should I seek farther store,
   And still make love anew?
When change itself can give no more,
   'Tis easy to be true.

123 *Chloris*

Chloris, I cannot say your eyes
Did my unwary heart surprise;
Nor will I swear it was your face,
Your shape, or any nameless grace;
For, you are so entirely fair,
To love a part injustice were:
No drowning man can know which drop
Of water his last breath did stop:
So when the stars in heaven appear,
And join to make the night look clear,
The light we no one's bounty call,
But the obliging gift of all.
He that does lips or hand adore,
Deserves them only and no more;
But I love all and every part,
And nothing less can ease my heart . . .

APHRA BEHN (1640–1689)

124 *A Coy Heart*

O what pleasure 'tis to find
   A coy heart melt by slow degrees!
When to yielding 'tis inclined,
   Yet, her fear a ruin sees;
When her tears do kindly flow
And her sighs do come and go.

O how charming 'tis to meet
   Soft resistance from the fair,
When her pride and wishes meet
   And by turns increase her care;
O How charming 'tis to know
She would yield but can't tell how!

O how pretty is her scorn
    When, confused 'twixt love and shame,
Still refusing, tho' she burn,
    The soft pressures of my flame!
Her pride in her denial lies
And mine is in my victories.

125 *Love in Fantastic Triumph Sate*

Love in fantastic triumph sate
    Whilst bleeding hearts around him flowed,
For whom fresh pains he did create
    And strange tyrannic power he showed:
From thy bright eyes he took his fires,
    Which round about in sport he hurled;
But 'twas from mine he took desires
    Enough t'undo the amorous world.

From me he took his sighs and tears,
    From thee his pride and cruelty;
From me his languishments and fears,
    And every killing dart from thee.
Thus thou and I the god have armed
    And set him up a deity;
But my poor heart alone is harmed,
    Whilst thine the victor is, and free!

126 *Pan, Grant that I May Never Prove*

Pan, grant that I may never prove
So great a Slave to fall in love,
And to an Unknown Deity
Resign my happy Liberty:
I love to see the Amorous Swains
    Unto my Scorn their Hearts resign:
With Pride I see the Meads and Plains
    Throng'd all with Slaves, and they all mine:
Whilst I the whining Fools despise,
That pay their Homage to my Eyes.

127   *Absent from Thee*

Absent from thee, I languish still;
   Then ask me not, when I return?
The straying fool 'twill plainly kill
   To wish all day, all night to mourn.

Dear! From thine arms then let me fly,
   That my fantastic mind may prove
The torments it deserves to try
   That tears my fixed heart from my love.

When, wearied with a world of woe,
   To thy safe bosom I retire
Where love and peace and truth doth flow,
   May I contented there expire,

Lest, once more wandering from that Heaven,
   I fall on some base heart unblest,
Faithless to thee, false, unforgiven,
   And lose my everlasting rest.

128 *While on Those Lovely Looks I Gaze*

While on those lovely looks I gaze,
    To see a Wretch persuing,
In Raptures of a blest amaze,
    His pleasing happy Ruine:
'Tis not for pity that I move;
    His Fate is too aspiring,
Whose Heart, broke with a load of Love,
    Dies wishing and admiring.

But if this Murder you'd forego,
    Your Slave from Death removing;
Let me your Art of Charming know,
    Or learn you mine of Loving.
But whether Life, or Death, betide,
    In Love 'tis equal Measure;
The Victor lives with empty Pride;
    The Vanquish'd die with Pleasure.

129   *My Dear Mistress Has a Heart*

My dear Mistress has a Heart
   Soft as those kind looks she gave me;
When with Love's resistless Art,
   And her Eyes she did enslave me.
But her Constancy's so weak,
   She's so wild, and apt to wander;
That my jealous Heart wou'd break,
   Should we live one day asunder.

Melting Joys about her move,
   Killing Pleasures, wounding Blisses;
She can dress her Eyes in Love,
   And her Lips can arm with Kisses.
Angels listen when she speaks,
   She's my delight, all Mankind's wonder:
But my jealous Heart would break,
   Should we live one day asunder.

JOHN WILMOT, EARL OF ROCHESTER

130 *Love and Life*

All my past life is mine no more;
  The flying hours are gone,
Like transitory dreams given o'er
Whose images are kept in store
  By memory alone.

Whatever is to come is not:
  How can it then be mine?
The present moment's all my lot,
And that, as fast as it is got,
  Phyllis, is wholly thine.

Then talk not of inconstancy,
  False hearts, and broken vows;
If I, by miracle, can be
This livelong minute true to thee,
  'Tis all that heaven allows.

131 *The Platonick Lady*

I could Love thee till I dye,
  Wouldst thou Love mee modestly;
And ne'er presse, while I live,
  For more than willingly I would give;
Which should sufficient be to prove
  I'de understand the Arte of Love.
I hate the thing is call'd Injoyment,
  Besydes it is a dull imployment,
It cutts of al that's Life and fler,
  From that which maybe term'd Desire.
Just Like the Bee whose sting is gon,
  Converts the owner to a Droane.

I Love a youth sho'd give me leave
    His Body in my Arms to wreath;
To presse him Gently and to kisse,
    To sigh and looke with Eyes that wish.
For what if I could once Obtaine,
    I would neglect with flatt disdaine
I'de give him Libertye to toye,
    And play with mee and court it Joye.
Our freedome should be full compleate,
    And nothing wanting but the feate:
Let's practice then, and we shall prove
    These are the only sweets of Love.

132 *To Corinna*

What Cruel Pains Corinna takes,
    To force that harmless frown;
When not one Charm her Face forsakes,
    Love cannot lose his own.

So sweet a Face, so soft a Heart,
    Such Eyes so very kind,
Betray, alas! the silly Art
    Virtue had ill design'd.

Poor feeble Tyrant! who in vain
    Would proudly take upon her,
Against kind Nature to maintain,
    Affected Rules of Honour.

The Scorn she bears so helpless proves,
    When I plead Passion to her,
That much she fears, (but more she loves,)
    Her Vassal should undo her.

133   *The Enchantment*

I did but look and love awhile,
   'Twas but for one half-hour:
Then to resist I had no will,
   And now I have no power.

To sigh and wish is all my case;
   Sighs which do heat impart
Enough to melt the coldest ice,
   Yet cannot warm your heart.

O would your pity give my heart
   One corner of your breast,
'Twould learn of yours the winning art,
   And quickly steal the rest.

JANE BARKER (1652–1727)

134 *To My Young Lover*

Incautious youth, why dost thou so misplace
Thy fine encomiums on an o'er-blown face;
Which after all the varnish of thy quill,
Its pristine wrinkles show apparent still:
Nor is it in the power of youth to move
An age-chilled heart to any strokes of love.
Then choose some budding beauty, which in time
May crown thy wishes in thy blooming prime:
For nought can make a more preposterous show,
Than April's flowers stuck on St Michael's bow.
To consecrate thy First-born sighs to me,
A superannuated deity;
Makes that idolatry and deadly sin,
Which otherwise had only venial been.

135   *That Field of Love*

I saw her stretched upon a flow'ry bank,
With her soft sorrows lulled into a slumber:
The summer's heat had to her nat'ral blush
Added a brighter and more tempting red:
The beauties of her neck, and naked breasts,
Lifted by inward starts, did rise and fall,
With motion that might put a soul in statue;
The matchless whiteness of her folded arms,
That seemed t'embrace the body whence they grew,
Fix'd me to gaze o'er all that field of love.
While to my ravished eyes officious wind,
Waving her robes, display'd such well turned limbs
As artists would in polished marble give
The wanton goddess, when supinely laid
She charms her gallant god to new enjoyment.

136   To Miss Charlotte Pulteney

(In her mother's arms)

Timely blossom, infant fair,
Fondling of a happy pair,
Every morn, and every night,
Their solicitous delight,
Sleeping, waking, still at ease,
Pleasing, without skill to please,
Little gossip, blithe and hale,
Tattling many a broken tale,
Singing many a tuneless song,
Lavish of a heedless tongue,
Simple maiden, void of art,
Babbling out the very heart,
Yet abandoned to thy will,
Yet imagining no ill,
Yet too innocent to blush,

Like the linnet in the bush,
To the mother-linnet's note
Moduling her slender throat,
Chirping forth thy petty joys,
Wanton in the change of toys,
Like the linnet green, in May,
Flitting to each bloomy spray,
Wearied then, and glad of rest,
Like the linnet in the nest.
This thy present happy lot,
This, in time, will be forgot:
Other pleasures, other cares,
Ever-busy Time prepares;
And thou shalt in thy daughter see,
This picture, once, resembled thee.

137   To Miss Margaret Pulteney

Dimply damsel, sweetly smiling,
All caressing, none beguiling,
Bud of beauty, fairly blowing,
Every charm to nature owing,
This and that new thing admiring,
Much of this and that enquiring,
Knowledge by degrees attaining,
Day by day some virtue gaining,
Ten years hence, when I leave chiming,
Beardless poets, fondly rhyming
(Fescu'd now, perhaps, in spelling),
On thy riper beauties dwelling,
Shall accuse each killing feature
Of the cruel, charming creature,
Whom I knew complying, willing,
Tender, and averse to killing.

138   *A Letter to Dafnis, 2 April 1685*

This to the Crown, and blessing of my life,
The much lov'd husband, of a happy wife.
To him, whose constant passion found the art
To win a stubborn, and ungrateful heart;
And to the World, by tend'rest proof discovers
They err, who say that husbands can't be lovers.
With such return of passion, as is due,
Daphnis I love, Daphnis my thoughts persue,
Daphnis, my hopes, my joys, are bounded all in you:
Ev'n I, for Daphnis, and my promise sake,
What I in women censure, undertake.
But this from love, not vanity, proceeds;
You know who writes; and I who 'tis that reads.
Judge not my passion, by my want of skill,
Many love well, though they express itt ill;
And I your censure cou'd with pleasure bear,
Wou'd you but soon return, and speak itt here.

139   *The Unequal Fetters*

Cou'd we stop the time that's flying
   Or recall it when 'tis past
Put far off the day of Dying
   Or make Youth forever last
To Love wou'd then be worth our cost.

But since we must loose those Graces
   Which at first your hearts have wonne
And you seek for in new Faces
   When our Spring of Life is done
It wou'd but urdge our ruine on

Free as Nature's first intention
   Was to make us, I'll be found
Nor by subtle Man's invention
   Yeild to be in Fetters bound
By one that walks a freer round.

Mariage does but slightly tye Men
    Whil'st close Pris'ners we remain
They the larger Slaves of Hymen
    Still are begging Love again
At the full length of all their chain.

140   *A Better Answer*

Dear Chloë, how blubbered is that pretty face!
    Thy cheek all on fire, and thy hair all uncurled:
Prithee quit this caprice; and, as old Falstaff says,
    Let us e'en talk a little like folks of this world.

How canst thou presume, thou hadst leave to destroy
    The beauties which Venus but lent to thy keeping?
Those looks were designed to inspire love and joy:
    More ordinary eyes may serve people for weeping.

To be vexed at a trifle or two that I writ,
    Your judgement at once, and my passion, you wrong:
You take that, for fact, which will scarce be found wit;
    Ods life! Must one swear to the truth of a song?

What I speak, my fair Chloë, and what I write, shows
    The difference there is betwixt nature and art:
I court others in verse – but I love thee in prose;
    And they have my whimsies – but thou has my heart.

The god of us verse-men, you know, child, the sun,
    How after his journeys he sets up his rest:
If at morning o'er earth 'tis his fancy to run;
    At night he declines on his Thetis's breast.

So when I am wearied with wandering all day,
    To thee, my delight, in the evening I come:
No matter what beauties I saw in my way,
    They were but my visits, but thou art my home.

Then finish, dear Chloë, this pastoral war;
    And let us like Horace and Lydia agree;
For thou art a girl as much brighter than her,
    As he was a poet sublimer than me.

141 *Soft Love, Spontaneous Tree*

Soft love, spontaneous tree, its parted root
Must from two hearts with equal vigour shoot;
Whilst each delighted and delighting gives
The pleasing ecstasy which each receives:
Cherished with hope, and fed with joy, it grows,
Its cheerful buds their op'ning bloom disclose
And round the happy soil diffusive odour flows.
If angry fate that mutual care denies,
The fading plant bewails its due supplies;
Wild with despair, or sick with grief, it dies.

142   *Remedia Amoris*
to Henry Cromwell Esq

Love and the gout invade the idle brain,
Bus'ness prevents the passion and the pain:
Ceres and Bacchus, envious of our case,
Blow up the flame, and heighten the disease.
Withdraw the fuel, and the fire goes out;
Hard beds, and fasting, cure both love and gout.

THOMAS PARNELL (1679–1718)

143   *When Thy Beauty Appears*

When thy beauty appears
In its graces and airs
All bright as an angel new dropped from the sky,
At distance I gaze and am awed by my fears:
So strangely you dazzle my eye!

But when without art
Your kind thoughts you impart,
When your love runs in blushes through every vein;
When it darts from your eyes, when it pants in your heart,
Then I know you're a woman again.

There's a passion and pride
In our sex (she replied),
And thus, might I gratify both, I would do:
Still an angel appear to each lover beside,
But still be a woman to you.

144 *The Caution*

Soft kisses may be innocent
But ah! Too easy maid, beware;
Tho' that is all thy kindness meant,
'Tis love's delusive, fatal snare.

No virgin e'er at first design'd
Thro' all the maze of love to stray;
But each new path allures her mind,
Till wandering on, she lose her way.

'Tis ere set out to stay;
But who the useful art can teach,
When sliding down a steepy way,
To stop, before the end we reach?

Keep ever something in thy power,
Beyond what would thy honour stain:
He will not dare to aim at more,
Who for small favours sighs in vain.

EDWARD LITTLETON (1680–1733)

145 Prudent Marriage

Let reason teach what passion fain would hide,
That Hymen's bands by prudence should be tied;
Venus in vain the wedded pair would crown,
If angry fortune on their union frown:
Soon will the flattering dream of bliss be o'er
And cloyed imagination cheat no more.
Then waking to the sense of lasting pain,
With mutual tears the nuptial couch they stain,
And that fond love, which should afford relief,
Does but increase the anguish of their grief,
While both could easier their own sorrows bear
Than the sad knowledge of each other's care.

LADY MARY WORTLEY MONTAGU (1684–1763)

146   Between Your Sheets

Between your sheets you soundly sleep
Nor dream of vigils that we lovers keep
While all the night, I waking sigh your name,
The tender sound does every nerve inflame,
Imagination shows me all your charms,
The plenteous silken hair, and waxen arms,
The well-turned neck, and snowy rising breast
And all the beauties that supinely rest between your sheets.
Ah Lindamira, could you see my heart,
How fond, how true, how free from fraudful art,
The warmest glances poorly do explain
The eager wish, the melting throbbing pain
Which through my very blood and soul I feel,
Which you cannot believe nor I reveal,
Which every metaphor must render less
And yet (methinks) which I could well express
                                        between your sheets.

LADY MARY WORTLEY MONTAGU

147 *The Lady's Resolve*
Written extempore on a window

While thirst of praise, and vain desire of fame,
In every age, is every woman's aim;
With courtship pleas'd, of silly toasters proud,
Fond of a train, and happy in a crowd;
On each proud fop bestowing some kind glance,
Each conquest owing to some loose advance;
While vain coquets affect to be pursu'd,
And think they're virtuous, if not grossly lewd:
Let this great maxim be my virtue's guide;
In part she is to blame that has been tried
He comes too near, that comes to be denied.

148 *On the Death of Mrs Bowes*

Hail, happy bride, for thou art truly blest!
Three months of rapture, crowned with endless rest.
Merit like yours was heaven's peculiar care,
You loved yet tasted happiness sincere.
To you the sweets of love were only shown,
The sure succeeding bitter dregs unknown;
You had not yet the fatal change deplored,
The tender lover for th'imperious lord:
Nor felt the pain that jealous fondness brings:
Nor felt that coldness from possession springs.
Above your sex, distinguished in your fate,
You trusted yet experienced no deceit;
Soft were your hours, and winged with pleasure flew;
No vain repentance gave a sigh to you:
And if superior bliss heaven can bestow,
With fellow angels you enjoy it now.

149   *Dear Colin*

Dear Colin, prevent my warm blushes,
  Since how can I speak without pain?
My eyes have oft told you my wishes,
  Oh! can't you their meaning explain?

My passion would lose by expression,
  And you too might cruelly blame;
Then don't you expect a confession
  Of what is too tender to name.

Since yours is the province of speaking,
  Why should you expect it from me?
Our wishes should be in our keeping,
  Till you tell us what they should be.

Then quickly why don't you discover?
  Did your heart feel such tortures as mine,
Eyes need tell over and over
  What I in my bosom confine.

ELIZABETH TAYLOR (1685–1722)

150   *Ye Virgin Powers! Defend My Heart*

Ye virgin powers! Defend my heart
   From amorous looks and smiles;
From saucy love, or nicer art
   Which most our sex beguiles.

From sighs, from vows, from awful fears
   That do to pity move;
From speaking-silence, and from tears,
   Those springs that water love.

But, if thro' passion I grow blind,
   Let honour be my guide;
And where frail nature seems inclined,
   There place a guard of pride.

A heart whose flames are seen, tho' pure,
   Needs every virtue's aid;
And those who think themselves secure,
   The soonest are betrayed.

SAMUEL JOHNSON (1709–1784)

151   *An Evening Ode – to Stella*

Ev'ning, now, from purple wings,
Sheds the grateful gifts she brings;
Brilliant drops bedeck the mead,
Cooling breezes shake the reed;
Shake the reed, and curl the stream,
Silver'd o'er with Cynthia's beam.
Near, the chequer'd, lonely grove
Hears, and keeps thy secrets, Love.
Stella! Thither let us stray,
Lightly o'er the dewy way;
Phœbus drives his burning car
Hence, my lovely Stella, far;
In his stead, the Queen of Night
Round us pours a lambent light;
Light that serves but just to show
Breasts that beat, and cheeks that glow.

Let us now, in whisper'd joy,
Ev'ning's silent hours employ:
Silence, best, and conscious shades
Please the hearts that Love invades;
Other pleasures give them pain,
Lovers all but Love disdain.

152 *An Ode on a Lady Leaving Her Place of Abode; Almost Impromptu*

When the departing sun resigns
The northern shores to clouds and frost
The chill inhabitant repines,
In half a year of darkness lost.

Cleora thus regretted flies,
Fair source of wit, and love, and mirth,
Withdraws the influence of those eyes,
Which gave a thousand pleasures birth.

Not long the happy Russians mourn;
Revolving springs their frosts repay.
O would Cleora thus return,
And bless me with continu'd day.

153   *An Evening Ode – Stella in Mourning*

When, lately, Stella's form displayd
The beauties of the gay brocade,
The nymphs, who found their pow'r decline,
Proclaim'd her, not so fair as fine.
'Fate! Snatch away the bright disguise,
And let the goddess trust her eyes.'
Thus blindly pray'd the fretful fair,
And fate malicious heard the pray'r.
But brightened by the sable dress,
As virtue rises in distress,
Since Stella still extends her reign,
Ah! How shall envy sooth her pain?
Th'adoring youth, and envious fair,
Henceforth shall form one common pray'r,
And Love and Hate alike implore
The skies, that Stella mourn no more.

154   *To a Young Lady on Her Birthday*

This tributary verse receive, my fair,
Warm with an ardent lover's fondest pray'r.
May this returning day for ever find
Thy form more lovely, more adorn'd thy mind;
All pains, all cares, may favouring heav'n remove,
All but the sweet solicitudes of love.
May powerful nature join with graceful art,
To point each glance, and force it to the heart.
O then, when conquer'd crowds confess thy sway,
When e'en proud wealth and prouder wit obey,
My fair, be mindful of the mighty trust,
Alas! 'Tis hard for beauty to be just.
Those sovereign charms with strictest care employ,
Nor give the generous pain, the worthless joy.

With his own form acquaint the forward fool,
Shewn in the faithful glass of ridicule;
Teach mimick censure, her own faults to find,
No more let coquets to themselves be blind,
So shall Belinda's charms improve mankind.

155   *To Lyce, an Elderly Lady*

Ye nymphs whom starry rays invest,
By flatt'ring poets giv'n;
Who shine, by lavish lovers drest,
In all the pomp of heav'n;

Engross not all the beams on high,
Which gild a lover's lays,
But as your sister of the sky,
Let Lyce share the praise.

Her silver locks display the moon,
Her brows a cloudy show,
Strip'd rainbows round her eyes are seen,
And show'rs from either flow.

Her teeth the night with darkness dyes,
She's starr'd with pimples o'er,
Her tongue like nimble lightning pines,
And can with thunder roar.

But some Zelinda while I sing
Denies my Lyce shines,
And all the pens of Cupid's wing
Attack my gentle lines.

Yet spite of fair Zelinda's eye,
And all her bards express,
My Lyce makes as good a sky,
And I but flatter less.

156   To Miss —

*On her giving the author a gold and silk
net-work purse of her own weaving*

Tho' gold and silk their charms unite,
To make thy curious web delight,
In vain the vary'd work would shine,
If wrought by any hand but thine;
Thy hand, that knows the subtler art,
To weave those nets that catch the heart;
Spread out by me, the roving coin
Thy nets may catch, but not confine;
Nor can I hope, thy silken chain
The glittering vagrants shall restrain.
Why, Sylvia, was it then decreed,
The heart, once caught, should ne'er be freed?

157   To Miss —

On her playing upon the harpsichord in a room
hung with some flower-pieces of her own painting

When Stella strikes the tuneful String
In Scenes of imitated Spring,
Where Beauty lavishes her Powers
On Beds of never-fading Flowers;
And Pleasure propagates around
Each Charm of modulated Sound;
Ah! think not, in the dang'rous hour,
The Nymph fictitious as the Flower;
But shun, rash Youth, the gay Alcove,
Nor tempt the Snares of wily Love.
When Charms thus press on every Sense,
What Thought of Flight, or of Defence?
Deceitful Hope, and vain Desire,
Forever flutter o'er her Lyre;
Delighting, as the Youth draws nigh,

To point the Glances of her Eye;
And forming with unerring Art,
New Chains to hold the Captive-Heart.
But on those Regions of Delight,
Might Truth intrude, with daring Flight,
Could Stella, sprightly, fair, and young,
One Moment hear the Moral Song,
Instruction with her Flowers might spring,
And Wisdom warble from her String.
Mark, when from thousand mingled Dyes
Thou seest one pleasing Form arise;
How active Light, and thoughtful Shade,
In greater Scenes each other aid;
Mark, when the dif'rent Notes agree
In friendly Contrariety;
How Passion's well-accorded Strife
Gives all the Harmony of Life:
Thy Pictures shall thy Conduct frame,
Consistent still, tho' not the same;
Thy Musick teach the nobler Art,
To tune the regulated Heart.

158 *To Mrs Thrale on Her Thirty-fifth Birthday*

Oft in Danger yet alive
We are come to Thirty-five,
Long may better Years arrive,
Better Years than Thirty-five;
Could Philosophers contrive
Life to stop at Thirty-five,
Time his Hours should never drive
O'er the Bounds of Thirty-five:
High to soar and deep to dive
Nature gives at Thirty-five;
Ladies – stock and tend your Hive,
Trifle not at Thirty-five:
For howe'er we boast and strive,
Life declines from Thirty-five
He that ever hopes to thrive
Must begin by Thirty-five:
And those who wisely wish to wive,
Must look on Thrale at Thirty-five.

159   *The Winter's Walk*

Behold my fair, where-e'er we rove,
    What dreary prospects round us rise,
The naked hills, the leafless grove,
    The hoary ground, the frowning skies.

Nor only through the wasted plain,
    Stern winter, is thy force contest,
Still wider spreads thy horrid reign,
    I feel thy pow'r usurp my breast.

Enliv'ning hope, and fond desire,
    Resign the heart to spleen and care,
Scarce frighted love maintains his fire,
    And rapture saddens to despair.

In groundless hope, and causeless fear,
  Unhappy man I behold thy doom,
    Still changing with the changeful year,
      The slave of sunshine and of gloom.

  Tir'd with vain joys, and false alarms,
    With mental and corporeal strife,
  Snatch me, my Stella, to thy arms,
    And screen me from the ills of life.

160 *Strephon, Your Breach of Faith and Trust*

Strephon, your breach of faith and trust
   Affords me no surprise;
A man who grateful was, or just.
   Might make my wonder rise.

That heart to you so fondly tied,
   With pleasure wore its chain,
But from your cold neglectful pride,
   Found liberty again.

For this no wrath inflames my mind,
   My thanks are due to thee;
Such thanks as gen'rous victors rind,
   Who set their captives free.

WILLIAM WHITEHEAD (1715–1785)

161 *The Je Ne Sais Quoi*

Yes, I'm in love, I feel it now,
    And Celia has undone me;
And yet I'll swear I can't tell how
    The pleasing plague stole on me.

'Tis not her face that love creates,
    For there no graces revel;
'Tis not her shape, for there the fates
    Have rather been uncivil.

'Tis not her shape, for sure in that,
    There's nothing more than common;
And all her sense is only chat,
    Like any other woman.

Her voice, her touch, might give th'alarm –
    'Tis both perhaps, or neither;
In short, 'tis that provoking charm
    Of Celia altogether.

DAVID GARRICK (1717–1779)

162   A Wife's Conquest

Ye fair married dames, who so often deplore,
That a lover once blessed is a lover no more;
Attend to my counsel, nor blush to be taught,
That prudence must cherish what beauty has caught.

The bloom of your cheek, and the glance of your eye,
Your roses and lilies may make the men sigh;
But roses and lilies and sighs pass away,
And passion will die as your beauties decay.

Use the man that you wed, like your favourite guitar,
Though music's in both, they are both apt to jar;
How tuneful and soft from a delicate touch,
Not handled too roughly, nor played on too much.

The sparrow and linnet will feed from your hand,
Grow tame by your kindness and come at command:
Exert with your husband the same happy skill;
For hearts, like your birds, may be tamed to your will.

Be gay and good-humoured, complying and kind;
Turn the chief of your care, from your face to your mind;
'Tis there that a wife may her conquest improve,
And Hymen shall rivet the fetters of love.

163   *Thou Genius of Connubial Love*

Thou genius of connubial love, attend!
Let silent wonder all thy powers suspend,
Whilst to thy glory I devote my lays,
And pour forth all my grateful heart in praise.
In lifeless strains let vulgar satire tell
That marriage oft is mixed with heaven and hell,
That conjugal delight is soured with spleen,
And peace and war compose the varied scene.
My muse a truth sublimer can assert,
And sing the triumphs of a mutual heart.

Thrice happy they who through life's varied tide
With equal pace and gentle motion glide,
Whom, though the wave of fortune sinks or swells,
One reason governs and one wish impels,

Whose emulation is to love the best,
Who feels no bliss but in each other blessed,
Who knows no pleasure but the joys they give,
Nor cease to love but when they cease to live.
If late these blessings in one lot combine,
Then let th'eternal page record them mine.

164   *What Torments Must the Virgin Prove*

What torments must the virgin prove
   That feels the pangs of hopeless love.
What endless cares must rack the breast
   That is by sure despair possessed.

When love in tender bosoms reigns,
   With all its soft, its pleasing pains,
Why should it be a crime to own
   The fatal flame we cannot shun?

The soul by nature formed sincere
   A slavish forced disguise must wear,
Lest the unthinking world reprove
   The heart that glows with generous love.

But oh! In vain the sigh's repressed,
    That gently heaves the pensive breast,
The glowing blush, the falling tear,
    The conscious wish, and silent fear.

Ye soft betrayers, aid my flame,
    And give my new desires a name;
Some power my gentle griefs redress,
    Reveal, or make my passion less.

OLIVER GOLDSMITH (1730–1774)

165 On seeing Mrs —— Perform in the Character of ——

To you bright fair the nine address their lays,
And tune my feeble voice to sing thy praise.
The heart-felt power of every charm divine,
Who can withstand their all-commanding shine?
See how she moves along with every grace
While soul-brought tears steal down each shining face,
She speaks, 'tis rapture all and nameless bliss,
Ye gods what transport e'er compar'd to this?
As when in Paphian groves the queen of love,
With fond complaint address'd the listening jove,
'Twas joy, and endless bosses all around,
And rocks forgot their hardness at the sound.
Then first, at last e'en Jove was taken in,
And felt her charms, without disguise, within.

166   *Addressed to a Young Lady*

Sweet stream, that winds through yonder glade,
Apt emblem of a virtuous maid –
Silent and chaste, she steals along,
Far from the world's gay, busy throng;
With gentle yet prevailing force,
Intent upon her destined course;
Graceful and useful all she does,
Blessing and blest, where'er she goes;
Pure blossomed, as that watery glass,
And heaven reflected in her face.

167 *Catharina*

addressed to Miss Stapleton (now Mrs Courtney)

She came – she is gone – we have met –
    And meet perhaps never again;
The sun of that Moment is set,
    And seems to have risen in vain.
Catharina has fled like a dream –
    (So vanishes pleasure, alas!)
But has left a regret and esteem
    That will not so suddenly pass.

The last evening ramble we made,
    Catharina, Maria, and I,
Our progress was often delayed
    By the nightingale warbling nigh.
We paused under rainy a tree,
    And much she was charmed with a tone,

Less sweet to Maria, and me,
　　Who so lately had witnessed her own.

My numbers that day she had sung,
　　And gave them a grace so divine,
As only her musical tongue
　　Could infuse into numbers of mine.
The longer I heard, I esteemed
　　The work of my fancy the more,
And e'en to myself never seemed
　　So tuneful a poet before.

Though the pleasures of London exceed
　　In number the days of the year,
Catharina, did nothing impede,
　　Would feel herself happier here;
For the close-woven arches of times
　　On the banks of our river, I know,
Are sweeter to her many times
　　Than aught that the city can show.

So it is when the mind is endued
    With a well-judging taste from above,
Then, whether embellished or rude,
    'Tis nature alone that we love.
The achievements of art may amuse,
    May even our wonder excite,
But groves, hills, and valleys diffuse
    A lasting, a sacred delight.

Since, then, in the rural recess
    Catharina alone can rejoice,
May it still be her lot to possess
    The scene of her sensible choice!
To inhabit a mansion remote
    From the clatter of street-pacing steeds,
And by Philomel's annual note
    To measure the life that she leads.

With her book, and her voice, and her lyre,
  To wing all her moments at home;
And with scenes that new rapture inspire,
  As oft, as it suits her to roam;
She will have just the life she prefers,
  With little to hope or to fear,
And ours would be pleasant as hers,
  Might we view her enjoying it here.

JOHN O'KEEFE (1747–1833)

168 *Amo, Amas, I Love a Lass*

Amo, amas,
  I love a lass
As a cedar tall and slender!
  Sweet cowslips' grace
  Is her Nominative Case
And she's of the Feminine Gender.

Rorum, corum, sunt Divorum!
  Harum scarum Divo!
Tag rag, merry derry, periwig and hatband,
  Hic, hac, horum Genetivo!

  Can I decline
  A Nymph divine?
Her voice as a flute is dulcis!
  Her oculi bright!

Her manus white!
And soft when I tacto, her pulse is!

Rorum, corum, sunt Divorum!
   Harum scarum Divo!
Tag rag, merry derry, periwig and hatband,
   Hic, hac, horum Genetivo!

   O, how bella
   Is my Puella!
I'll kiss sœculorum!
   If I've luck, Sir!
   She's my Uxor!
O, dies benedictorum!

Rorum, corum, sunt Divorum!
   Harum scarum Divo!
Tag rag, merry derry, periwig and hatband,
   Hic, hac, horum Genetivo!

169 *Epilogue*

Here lies a nymph! Whose beauty was her bane,
Whose mind, in virtue's school, was taught in vain,
That outward charms acquire more excellence,
When ruled by chastity, and innocence:
She loved a youth, beyond her love of fame,
For him, disgraced the splendour of her name,
And when he ceased with partial eyes to view
Her charms, she gladly from the world withdrew . . .
May other nymphs, by her disgrace, forbear
To think their faces will continue fair,
Their lovers constant, or their friends sincere
Beauty is doomed to be of transient date,
And love is oft the harbinger of hate,
At best, indifference coldly steps between,
Whilst sorrow calls on death to close the scene:
Then must the fading form lose all its grace,

And ev'ry blooming charm desert the face,
The broken heart shall rapidly decay,
And all the dreams of pleasure pass away,
The pulse shall cease to beat, the eye to weep,
And ev'ry trouble in the grave shall sleep . . .

WILLIAM BLAKE (1757–1827)

170 *The Clod and the Pebble*

'Love seeketh not itself to please,
Nor for itself bath any care,
But for another gives its ewe,
And builds a heaven in hell's despair.'

So sung a little clod of clay,
Trodden with the cattle's feet,
But a pebble of the brook
Warbled out these metres meet:

'Love seeketh only self to please,
To bind another to its delight,
Joys in another's loss of ease,
And builds a hell in heaven's despite.'

171   *The Garden of Love*

I went to the garden of love,
And saw what I never had seen:
A chapel was built in the midst,
Where I used to play on the green.

And the gates of this chapel were shut,
And 'Thou shalt not' writ over the door;
So I turned to the garden of love
That so many sweet flowers bore;

And I saw it was fillèd with graves,
And tomb-stones where flowers should be;
And priests in black gowns were walking
                                    their rounds,
And binding with briars my joys and desires.

172   *Infant Joy*

'I have no name:
I am but two days old.'
What shall I call thee?
'I happy am,
Joy is my name.'
Sweet joy befall thee!

Pretty joy!
Sweet joy but two days old,
Sweet joy I call thee:
Thou dost smile,
I sing the while,
Sweet joy befall thee!

173   *Love that Never Told Can Be*

Never seek to tell thy love,
   Love that never told can be;
For the gentle wind doth move
   Silently, invisibly;

I told my love, I told my love,
   I told her all my heart;
Trembling, cold, in ghastly fears.
   Ah! she did depart!

Soon after she was gone from me,
   A traveller came by,
Silently, invisibly:
   He took her with a sigh.

174   *My Pretty Rose Tree*

A flower was offered to me,
Such a flower as May never bore;
But I said 'I've a pretty rose-tree,'
And I passèd the sweet flower o'er.

Then I went to my pretty rose-tree,
To tend her by day and by night.
But my rose turned away with jealousy,
And her thorns were my only delight.

175   *The Lamb*

Little Lamb, who made thee?
Dost thou know who made thee?
Gave thee life, and bid thee feed
By the stream and o'er the mead;
Gave thee clothing of delight,
Softest clothing, woolly, bright;
Gave thee such a tender voice,
Making all the vales rejoice?
Little Lamb, who made thee?
Dost thou know who made thee?

Little Lamb, I'll tell thee,
Little Lamb, I'll tell thee:
He is callèd by thy name,
For He calls himself a Lamb.

He is meek, and He is mild;
He became a little child.
I, a child, and thou a lamb,
We are cabled by His name.
  Little Lamb, God bless thee!
  Little Lamb, God bless thee!

ROBERT BURNS (1759–1796)

176 *O, My Luve's Like a Red, Red Rose*

O, my luve's like a red, red rose,
   That's newly sprung in June:
O, my luve's like the melodie
   That's sweetly played in tune.

As fair art thou, my bonnie lass,
   So deep in luve am I:
And I will luve thee still, my dear,
   Till a' the seas gang dry.

Till a' the seas gang dry, my dear,
   And the rocks melt wi' the sun:
I will luve thee still, my dear,
   While the sands o' life shall run.

And fare thee weel, my only luve,
   And fare thee weel awhile!
And I will come again, my luve,
   Tho' it were ten thousand mile.

177 *Highland Mary*

Ye banks and braes and streams around
   The castle o' Montgomery,
Green be your woods, and fair your flowers,
   Your waters never drumlie!
There simmer first unfalds her robes,
   And there the largest tarry;
For there I took the last fareweel
   O' my sweet Highland Mary.

How sweetly bloomed the gay green birk,
   How rich the hawthorn's blossom,
As, underneath their fragrant shade,
   I clasped her to my bosom!
The golden hours, on angel wings,
   Flew o'er me and my dearie;
For dear to me as light and life
   Was my sweet Highland Mary.

Wi' mony a vow and locked embrace
    Our parting was fu' tender;
And, pledging aft to meet again,
    We tore oursels asunder;
But oh! Fell Death's untimely frost,
    That nipt my flower sae early!
Now green's the sod and cauld's the clay
    That wraps my Highland Mary.

Oh, pale, pale now those rosy lips,
    I aft hae kissed so fondly!
And closed for aye the sparkling glance
    That dwelt on me see kindly;
And mouldering now in silent dust
    That heart that lo'ed me dearly!
But still within my bosom's core
    Shall live my Highland Mary.

178 *Ae Fond Kiss*

Ae fond kiss, and when we sever, –
Ae faerweel, and then – for ever!
Deep in heart-wrung tears I'll pledge thee!
Warring sighs and groans I'll wage thee!

Who shall say that fortune grieves him,
While the star of hope she leaves him?
Me, nae cheerfu' twinkle lights me, –
Dark despair around benights me.

I'll ne'er blame my partial fancy,
Naething could resist my Nancy;
But to see her was to love her –
Love but her, and love for ever.

Had we never lov'd sae kindly –
Had we never lov'd sae blindly –
Never met – or never parted,
We had ne'er been broken-hearted!

Fare-thee-weel, thou first and fairest!
Fare-thee-weel, thou best and dearest!
Thine be ilka joy and treasure,
Peace, enjoyment, love, and pleasure!

Ae fond kiss, and then we sever
Ae fareweel, alas! for ever!
Deep in heart-wrung tears I'll pledge thee!
Warring sighs and groans I'll wage thee!

179 *Once Fondly Loved*

Once fondly loved, and still remembered dear,
  Sweet early object of my youthful vows.
Accept this mark of friendship, warm, sincere –
  Friendship! 'tis all cold duty now allows:

And when you read the simple, artless rhymes,
  One friendly sigh for him – he asks no more –
Who distant burns in flaming torrid climes,
  Or haply lies beneath th' Atlantic roar.

180   *To Cupid*

Child, with many a childish wile,
Timid look, and blushing smile,
Downy wings to steal thy way,
Gilded bow, and quiver gay,
Who in thy simple mien would trace
The tyrant of the human race?

Who is he whose flinty heart
Hath not felt the flying dart?
Who is he that from the wound
Hath not pain and pleasure found?
Who is he that hath not shed
Curse and blessing on thy head?

FRANK SAYERS (1763–1817)

181 *Thy Perfect Mind*

What tho' I'm told that Flora's face
    Is flush'd with fresher tints than thine;
That Chloë moves with nobler grace;
    That Laura's lightnings brighter shine:

What tho' I'm told Zelinda's breast
    Is whiter than the mountain-snows;
That Fulvia's lips, in dimples drest,
    Are sweeter than the summer rose:

For ever hanging on thy smile,
    To others' charms my soul is blind:
What perfect form can him beguile?
    Who doats upon thy perfect mind.

CATHERINE MARIA FANSHAWE (1765–1834)

182   *When Last We Parted*

When last we parted, thou wert young and fair,
    How beautiful let fond remembrance say!
    Alas! Since then old time has stolen away
Full thirty years, leaving my temples bare.
So has it perished like a thing of air,
    The dream of love and youth! Now both are grey
    Yet still remembering that delightful day,
Though time with his cold touch has blanched
                                        my hair,
Though I have suffered many years of pain
    Since then, though I did never think to live
To hear that voice or see those eyes again,
    I can a sad but cordial greeting give,
        And for thy welfare breathe as warm a prayer
        As when I loved thee young and fair.

183   *Lucy*

She dwelt among the untrodden ways
   Beside the springs of Dove,
A Maid whom there were none to praise
   And very few to love:

A violet by a mossy stone
   Half hidden from the eye!
– Fair as a star, when only one
   Is shining in the sky.

She lived unknown, and few could know
   When Lucy ceased to be;
But she is in her grave, and, oh,
   The difference to me!

184   *A Perfect Woman*

She was a phantom of delight
When first she gleamed upon my sight;
A lovely apparition, sent
To be a moment's ornament;
Her eyes as stars of twilight fair;
Like twilight's, too, her dusky hair;
But all things else about her drawn
From May-time and the cheerful dawn;
A dancing shape, an image gay,
To haunt, to startle, and waylay.

I saw her upon nearer view,
A spirit, yet a woman too!
Her household motions light and free,
And steps of virgin-liberty;

A countenance in which did meet
Sweet records, promises as sweet ;
A creature not too bright or good
For human nature's daily food,
For transient sorrows, simple wiles,
Praise, blame, love, kisses, tears, and smiles,

And now I see with eye serene
The very pulse of the machine;
A being breathing thoughtful breath,
A traveller between life and death :
The reason firm, the temperate will,
Endurance, foresight, strength, and skill;
A perfect woman, nobly planned
To warn, to comfort, and command;
And yet a spirit still, and bright
With something of an angel-light.

185   *The Maid of Neidpath*

O lovers' eyes are sharp to see,
   And lovers' ears in hearing;
And love, in life's extremity,
   Can lend an hour of cheering.
Disease had been in Mary's bower,
   And slow decay from mourning.
Though now she sits on Neidpath's Tower,
   To watch her love's returning.

All sunk and dim her eyes so bright,
   Her form decayed by pining,
Till through her wasted hand, at night,
   You saw the taper shining;
By fits, a sultry hectic hue
   Across her cheek was flying,
By fits, so ashy pale she grew,
   Her maidens thought her dying.

Yet keenest powers to see and hear
   Seemed in her frame residing;
Before the watch-dog prick'd his ear
   She heard her lover's riding;
Ere scarce a distant form was ken'd,
   She knew, and waved to greet him;
And o'er the battlement did bend,
   As on the wing to meet him.

He came – he passed – an heedless gaze,
   As o'er some stranger glancing;
Her welcome, spoke in faltering phrase,
   Lost in his courser's prancing.
The castle arch, whose hollow tone
   Returns each whisper spoken,
Could scarcely catch the feeble moan
   Which told her heart was broken.

186　Woman's Faith

Woman's faith, and woman's trust –
Write the characters in dust;
Stamp them on the running stream,
Print them on the moon's pale beam,
And each evanescent letter
Shall be clearer, firmer, better,
And more permanent, I ween,
Than the thing those letters mean.

I have strained the spider's thread
'Gainst the promise of a maid;
I have weighed a grain of sand
'Gainst her plight of heart and hand;
I told my true love of the token,
How her faith proved light, and her word
　　　　　　　　　　　　was broken:
Again her word and truth she plight,
And I believed them again ere night.

187 *The Exchange*

We pledged our hearts, my love and I, –
　　I in my arms the maiden clasping;
I could not guess the reason why,
　　But, oh! I trembled like an aspen.

Her father's love she bade me gain;
　　I went, but shook like any reed!
I strove to act the man – in vain!
　　We had exchanged our hearts indeed.

188   *Farewell to Love*

Farewell, sweet Love! Yet blame you not my truth;
  More fondly ne'er did mother eye her child
Than I your form: yours were my hopes of youth,
  And as you shaped my thoughts I sighed or smiled.

While most were wooing wealth, or gaily swerving
  To pleasure's secret haunts, and some apart
Stood strong in pride, self-conscious of deserving,
  To you I gave my whole weak wishing heart.

And when I met the maid that realized
  Your fair creations, and had won her kindness,
Say, but for her if aught on earth I prized!
  Your dreams alone I dreamt, and caught your blindness.

O grief! – But farewell, Love! I will go play me
With thoughts that please me less, and less betray me.

189   *The Happy Husband – a Fragment*

Oft, oft methinks, the while with thee,
    I breathe, as from the heart, thy dear
    And dedicated name, I hear
A promise and a mystery,
    A pledge of more than passing life,
    Yea, in that very name of Wife!

A pulse of love, that ne'er can sleep I
    A feeling that upbraids the heart
    With happiness beyond desert,
That gladness half requests to weep I
    Nor bless I not the keener sense
    And unalarming turbulence

Of transient joys, that ask no sting
    From jealous fears, or coy denying;
    But born beneath Love's brooding wing,

And into tenderness soon dying,
   Wheel out their giddy moment, then
   Resign the soul to love again;

A more precipitated vein
   Of notes, that eddy in the flow
   Of smoothest song, they come, they go,
And leave their sweeter understrain
   Its own sweet self – a love of Thee
   That seems, yet cannot greater be!

190 *The Presence of Love*

And in Life's noisiest hour,
Their whispers still the ceaseless Love of Thee,
The heart's Self-solace and soliloquy.

You mould my Hopes, you fashion me within;
And to the leading Love-throb in the Heart
Thro' all my Being all my pulses beat.
You lie in all my many Thoughts, like Light,
Like the fair light of Dawn, or summer-Eve
On rippling Stream, or cloud-reflecting Lake.

And looking to the Heaven, that bends above you
How oft I bless the Lot, that made me love you.

SAMUEL TAYLOR COLERIDGE

191   To a Young Lady

(Miss Lavinia Poole) on her recovery from a fever

> Why need I say, Louisa dear!
> How glad I am to see you here,
>   A lovely convalescent;
> Risen from the bed of pain and fear,
>   And feverish heat incessant.
>
> The sunny showers, the dappled sky,
> The little birds that warble high,
>   Their vernal loves commencing,
> Will better welcome you than I
>   With their sweet influencing.

Believe me, while in bed you lay,
Your danger taught us all to pray:
    You made us grow devouter!
Each eye looked up and seemed to say,
    How can we do without her?

Besides, what vexed us worse, we knew,
They have no need of such as you
    In the place where you were going:
This World has angels all too few,
    And Heaven is overflowing!

192   *Water Ballad – from the French*

'Come hither, gently rowing,
   Come, bear me quickly o'er
This stream so brightly flowing
   To yonder woodland shore.
But vain were my endeavour
   To pay thee, courteous guide;
Row on, row on, for ever
   I'd have thee by my side.

'Good boatman, prithee haste thee,
   I seek my father-land.'
'Say, when I there have placed thee,
   Dare I demand thy hand?'
'A maiden's head can never
   So hard a point decide;
Row on, row on, for ever
   I'd have thee by my side.'

The happy bridal over
   The wanderer ceased to roam,
For, seated by her lover,
   The boat became her home.
And still they sang together
   As steering o'er the tide:
'Row on through wind and weather
   For ever by my side.'

193 A New Feeling

'Twas a new feeling – something more
Than we had dared to own before,
  Which then we hid not;
We saw it in each other's eye,
And wished, in every half-breathed sigh,
  To speak, but did not.

She felt my lips' impassioned touch –
'Twas the first time I dared so much,
  And yet she chid not;
But whispered o'er my burning brow,
'Oh, do you doubt I love you now?'
  Sweet soul! I did not.

Warmly I felt her bosom thrill,
I pressed it closer, closer still,
   Though gently bid not;
Till – oh! The world hath seldom heard
Of lovers, who so nearly erred,
   And yet, who did not.

194   *The Kiss*

Give me, my love, that billing kiss
　　I taught you one delicious night,
When, turning epicures in bliss,
　　We tried inventions of delight.

Come, gently steal my lips along,
　　And let your lips in murmurs move,
Ah, no I – again – that kiss was wrong –
　　How can you be so dull, my love?

'Cease, cease!' the blushing girl replied –
　　And in her milky arms she caught me –
'How can you thus your pupil chide;
　　You know 'twas in the dark you taught me!'

195   *Rondeau*

Jenny kissed me when we met,
　Jumping from the chair she sat in;
Time, you thief, who love to get
　Sweets into your list, put that in!
Say I'm weary, say I'm sad,
　Say that health and wealth have missed me,
Say I'm growing old, but add,
　Jenny kissed me.

196 *She Walks in Beauty*

I

She walks in beauty, like the night
  Of cloudless climes and starry skies;
And all that's best of dark and bright
  Meet in her aspect and her eyes:
Thus mellowed to that tender light
  Which heaven to gaudy day denies.

II

One shade the more, one ray the less,
  Had half impaired the nameless grace
Which waves in every raven tress,
  Or softly lightens o'er her face;
Where thoughts serenely sweet express
  How pure, how dear their dwelling-place.

III

And on that cheek, and o'er that brow,
   So soft, so calm, yet eloquent,
The smiles that win, the tints that glow,
   But tell of days in goodness spent,
A mind at peace with all below,
   A heart whose love is innocent!

197   *Love's Philosophy*

The fountains mingle with the river
   And the rivers with the ocean,
The winds of heaven mix for ever
   With a sweet emotion;
Nothing in the world is single;
   All things by a law divine
In one spirit meet and mingle.
   Why not I with thine? –
See the mountains kiss high heaven
   And the waves clasp one another;
No sister-flower would be forgiven
   If it disdained its brother;
And the sunlight clasps the earth
   And the moonbeams kiss the sea:
What is all this sweet work worth
   If thou kiss not me?

198   *First Love*

I ne'er was struck before that hour,
  With love so sudden and so sweet.
Her face it bloomed like a sweet flower,
  And stole my heart away complete.
My face turned pale a deadly pale,
  My legs refused to walk away,
And when she looked what could I ail,
  My life and all seemed turned to clay.

And then my blood rushed to my face,
  And took my eyesight quite away.
The trees and bushes round the place,
  Seemed midnight at noon day.
I could not see a single thing,
  Words from my eyes did start.
They spoke as chords do from the sting,
  And blood burnt round my heart.

Are flowers the winter's choice?
   Is love's bed always snow?
She seemed to hear my silent voice,
   Not love's appeals to know.
I never saw so sweet a face
   As that I stood before.
My heart has left its dwelling place
   And can return no more.

199   *O Love is So Deceiving*

O love is so deceiving
Like bees it wears a sting.
I thought it true believing
But it's no such thing.
They smile but to deceive you
They kiss and then they leave you
Speak truth they won't believe you
Their honey wears a sting.

What's the use o' pretty faces
Ruby lips and cheeks so red?
Flowers grow in pleasant places
So does a maidenhead.
The fairest won't believe you,
The foulest all deceive you,
The many laugh and grieve you
Until your coffin dead.

200   *Say What is Love*

Say what is love – to live in vain
To live and die and live again

Say what is love – is it to be
In prison still and still be free

Or seem as free – alone and prove
The hopeless hopes of real love?

Does real love on earth exist?
'Tis like a sunbeam on the mist

That fades and nowhere will remain
And nowhere is o'ertook again.

Say what is love – a blooming name
A rose leaf on the page of fame

That blooms then fades – to cheat no more
And is what nothing was before.

Say what is love – what e'er it be
It centres, Mary, still with thee.

201 Sweet in Her Green Dell the Flower of Beauty Slumbers

Sweet in her green dell the flower of beauty slumbers,
    Lulled by the faint breezes sighing through her hair;
Sleeps she and hears not the melancholy numbers
    Breathed to my sad lute 'mid the lonely air.

Down from the high cliffs the rivulet is teeming
    To wind round the willow banks that lure him
                            from above:
O that in tears, from my rocky prison streaming,
    I too could glide to the bower of my love!

Ah! where the woodbines with sleepy arms have
                             wound her,
    Opes she her eyelids at the dream of my lay,

Listening, like the dove, while the Mountains echo
                                    round her,
   To her lost mate's call in the forests far away.

Come then, my bird! For the peace thou ever bearest,
   Still Heaven's messenger of comfort to me
Come this fond bosom, O faithfullest and fairest,
   Bleeds with its death-wound, its wound of love for thee!

202   *Love*

O Love! what art thou, Love? the ace of hearts,
Trumping earth's kings and queens, and all its suits
A player, masquerading many parts
In life's odd carnival; – A boy that shoots,
From ladies' eyes, such mortal woundy darts;
A gardener, pulling heartsease up by the roots;
The Puck of Passion – partly false – part real –
A marriageable maiden's 'beau-ideal'.

O Love! what art thou, Love? a wicked thing,
Making green misses spoil their work at school;
A melancholy man, cross-gartering?
Grave ripe-faced wisdom made an April fool?
A youngster tilting at a wedding-ring?
A sinner, sitting on a cuttie stool?
A Ferdinand de Something in a hovel,
Helping Matilda Rose to make a novel?

O Love! what art thou, Love? one that is bad
With palpitations of the heart-like mine –
A poor bewildered maid, making so sad
A necklace of her garters-fell design
A poet, gone unreasonably mad,
Ending his sonnets with a hempen line ?
O Love! – but whither now? forgive me, pray;
I'm not the first that Love hath led astray.

203 *Love, Dearest Lady*

Love, dearest lady, such as I would speak,
Lives not within the humour of the eye;
Not being but an outward phantasy,
That skims the surface of a tinted cheek, –
Else it would wane with beauty, and grow weak,
As if the rose made summer, – and so lie
Amongst the perishable things that die,
Unlike the love which I would give and seek,
Whose health is of no hue – to feel decay
With cheeks' decay, that have a rosy prime.
Love is its own great loveliness alway,
And takes new lustre from the touch of time;
Its bough owns no December and no May,
But bears its blossom into Winter's clime.

204 *To Fancy*

Most delicate Ariel! submissive thing,
Won by the mind's high magic to its hest, –
Invisible embassy, or secret guest, –
Weighing the light air on a lighter wing
Whether into the midnight moon, to bring
Illuminate visions to the eye of rest, –
Or rich romances from the florid West, –
Or to the sea, for mystic whispering, –
Still by thy charmed allegiance to the will,
The fruitful wishes prosper in the brain,
As by the fingering of fairy skill, –
Moonlight, and waters, and soft music's strain,
Odours, and blooms, and my Miranda's smile,
Making this dull world an enchanted isle.

205 *On a Picture of Hero and Leander*

Why, Love, why
Such a water-rover?
Would she love thee more
For coming half-seas over?

Why. Lady, why
So in love with dipping?
Must a lad of Greece
Come all over dripping?

Why, Cupid, why
Make the passage brighter?
Were not any boat
Better than a lighter?

Why, Maiden, why
So intrusive standing?
Must thou be on the stair
When he is on the landing?

ELIZABETH BARRETT BROWNING (1806–61)

206   *Go From Me*

Go from me. Yet I feel that I shall stand
Henceforward in thy shadow. Nevermore
Alone upon the threshold of my door
Of individual life I shall command
The uses of my soul, nor lift my hand
Serenely in the sunshine as before,
Without the sense of that which I forbore –
Thy touch upon the palm. The widest land
Doom takes to part us, leaves thy heart in mine
With pulses that beat double. What I do
And what I dream include thee, as the wine
Must taste of its own grapes. And when I sue
God for myself, He hears that name of thine.
And sees within my eyes the tears of two.

from *Sonnets from the Portuguese* VI

207   *What Can I Give Thee Back?*

What can I give thee back, O liberal
And princely giver, who hast brought the gold
And purple of thine heart, unstained, untold,
And laid them on the outside of the wall
For such as I to take to leave withal,
In unexpected largesse? Am I cold,
Ungrateful, that for these most manifold
High gifts, I render nothing back at all?
Not so; not cold, – but very poor instead.
Ask God who knows. For frequent tears have run
The colours from my life, and left so dead
And pale a stuff, it were not fitly done
To give the same as pillow to thy head
Go farther! let it serve to trample on.

from *Sonnets from the Portuguese* VIII

208   *Can It Be Right?*

Can it be right to give what I can give?
To let thee sit beneath the fall of tears
As salt as mine, and hear the sighing years
Re-sighing on my lips renunciative
Through those infrequent smiles which fail to live
For all thy adjurations? O my fears,
That this can scarce be right! We are not peers,
So to be lovers; and I own, and grieve,
That givers of such gifts as mine are, must
Be counted with the ungenerous. Out, alas!
I will not soil thy purple with my dust,
Nor breathe my poison on thy Venice-glass,
Nor give thee any love – which were unjust.
Beloved, I only love thee! let it pass.

from *Sonnets from the Portuguese* IX

209 *Beautiful Love*

Yet, love, mere love, is beautiful indeed
And worthy of acceptation. Fire is bright,
Let temple burn, or flax; an equal light
Leaps in the flame from cedar-plank or weed:
And love is fire. And when I say at need
I love thee . . . mark! . . . I love thee – in thy sight
I stand transfigured, glorified aright,
With conscience of the new rays that proceed
Out of my face toward thine. There's nothing low
In love, when love the lowest: meanest creatures
Who love God, God accepts while loving so.
And what I feel, across the inferior features
Of what I am, cloth flash itself, and show
How that great work of Love enhances Nature's.

from *Sonnets from the Portuguese* x

210　*The Love I Bear Thee*

And wilt thou have me fashion into speech
The love I bear thee, finding words enough,
And hold the torch out, while the winds are rough,
Between our faces, to cast light on each?
I drop it at thy feet. I cannot teach
my hand to hold my spirit so far off
From myself . . . me . . . that I should bring thee proof
In words, of love hid in me out of reach.
Nay, let the silence of my womanhood
Commend my woman-love to thy belief,
Seeing that I stand unwon, however wooed,
And rend the garment of my life, in brief,
By a most dauntless, voiceless fortitude,
Let one touch of this heart convey its grief.

from *Sonnets from the Portuguese* XIII

211   *Say Thou Dost Love Me*

Say over again, and yet once over again,
That thou dost love me. Though the word repeated
Should seem 'a cuckoo-song,' as thou dost treat it,
Remember, never to the hill or plain,
Valley and wood, without her cuckoo-strain
Comes the fresh Spring in all her green completed.
Belovèd, I, amid the darkness greeted
By a doubtful spirit-voice, in that doubt's pain
Cry, 'Speak once more – thou lovest!' Who can fear
Too many stars, though each in heaven shall roll,
Too many flowers, though each shall crown the year?
Say thou dost love me, love me, love me - toll
The silver iterance! – only minding, Dear,
To love me also in silence with thy soul.

from *Sonnets from the Portuguese* XXII

212   *Two Souls Face to Face*

When our two souls stand up erect and strong,
Face to face, silent, drawing nigh and nigher,
Until the lengthening wings break into fire
At either curvèd point, – what bitter wrong
Can the earth do to us, that we should not long
Be here contented? Think. In mounting higher,
The angels would press on us and aspire
To drop some golden orb of perfect song
Into our deep, dear silence. Let us stay
Rather on earth, Belovèd, – where the unfit
Contrarious moods of men recoil away
And isolate pure spirits, and permit
Aplace to stand and love in for a day,
With darkness and the death-hour rounding it.

from *Sonnets from the Portuguese* XXII

213   *First Time He Kissed Me*

First time he kissed me, he but only kissed
The fingers of this hand wherewith I write;
And ever since, it grew more clean and white,
Slow to world-greetings, quick with its 'Oh, list,'
When the angels speak. A ring of amethyst
I could not wear here, plainer to my sight,
Than that first kiss. The second passed in height
The first, and sought the forehead, and half missed,
Half falling on the hair. O beyond meed!
That was the chrism of love, which love's own crown,
With sanctifying sweetness, did precede.
The third upon my lips was folded down
In perfect, purple state; since when, indeed,
I have been proud and said, 'My love, my own.'

from *Sonnets from the Portuguese* XXXVIII

214   *How Do I Love Thee?*

How do I love thee? Let me count the ways.
I love thee to the depth and breadth and height
My soul can reach, when feeling out of sight
For the ends of Being and ideal Grace.
I love thee to the level of every day's
Most quiet need, by sun and candlelight.
I love thee freely, as men strive for Right;
I love thee purely, as they turn from Praise.
I love thee with the passion put to use
In my old griefs, and with my childhood's faith.
I love thee with a love I seemed to lose
With my lost saints – I love thee with the breath,
Smiles, tears, of all my life! – and, if God choose,
I shall but love thee better after death.

from *Sonnets from the Portuguese* XLIII

CAROLINE NORTON (1808–77)

215 *Where the Red-Wine Cup Floweth*

Where the red wine-cup floweth, there art thou!
Where luxury curtains out the evening sky; –
Triumphant Mirth sits flush'd upon thy brow,
And ready laughter lurks within thine eye.
Where the long day declineth, lone I sit,
In idle thought, my listless hands entwined,
And, faintly smiling at remembered wit,
Act the scene over to my musing mind.
In my lone dreams I hear thy eloquent voice,
I see the pleased attention of the throng,
And bid my spirit in thy joy rejoice,
Lest in love's selfishness I do thee wrong.
Ah! midst that proud and mirthful company
Send'st thou no wondering thought to love and me?

216 *O That 'Twere Possible*

O that 'twere possible
After long grief and pain
To find the arms of my true love
Round me once again! . . .

A shadow flits before me,
Not thou. but like to thee:
Ah, Christ! that it were possible
For one short hour to see
The souls we loved, that they might tell us
What and where they be!

217   FROM *The Princess*

Now sleeps the crimson petal, now the white;
Nor waves the cypress in the palace walk;
Nor winks the gold fin in the porphyry font:
The firefly wakens: waken thou with me.

   Now droops the milkwhite peacock like a ghost,
And like a ghost she glimmers on to me.

   Now lies the earth all Danaë to the stars,
And all thy heart lies open unto me.

   Now slides the silent meteor on, and leaves
A shining furrow, as thy thoughts in me.

   Now folds the lily all her sweetness up,
And slips into the bosom of the lake:
So Cold thyself, my dearest, thou, and slip
Into my bosom and be lost in me.

218   A Petition

Lady, whom my belovèd loves so well!
   When on his clasping arm thy head reclineth,
When on thy lips his ardent kisses dwell,
   And the bright flood of burning light that shineth
In his dark eyes, is pourèd into thine;
   When thou shalt lie enfolded to his heart
In all the trusting helplessness of love;
   If in such joy sorrow can find a part,
Oh, give one sigh unto a doom like mine!
   Which I would have thee pity, but not prove.
One cold, calm, careless, wintry look that fell
   Haply by chance on one, is all that he
Ever gave my love; round that, my wild thoughts dwell
   In one eternal pang of memory.

219 My Love

There's not a fibre in my trembling frame
   That does not vibrate when thy step draws near,
   There's not a pulse that throbs not when I hear
Thy voice, thy breathing, nay thy very name.
   When thou art with me every sense seems dim,
   And all I am, or know, or feel is thee;
My soul grows faint, my veins run liquid flame,
   And my bewildered spirit seems to swim
   In eddying whirls of passion, dizzily.
When thou art gone, there creeps into my heart
   A cold and bitter consciousness of pain:
The light, the warmth of life with thee depart,
   And I sit dreaming over and over again
Thy greeting clasp, thy parting look and tone;
And suddenly I wake – and I am alone.

220 *The Owl and The Pussy-cat*

The Owl and the Pussy-cat went to sea
   In a beautiful pea-green boat,
They took some honey, and plenty of money,
   Wrapped up in a five-pound note.
The Owl looked up to the stars above,
   And sang to a small guitar,
'O lovely Pussy! O Pussy, my love,
  What a beautiful Pussy you are,
   You are,
   You are!
  What a beautiful Pussy you are!'

Pussy said to the Owl, 'You elegant fowl!
   How charmingly sweet you sing!
O let us be married! Too long we have tarried:
   But what shall we do for a ring?'

They sailed away, for a year and a day,
    To the land where the Bong-tree grows
And there in a wood a Piggy-wig stood
    With a ring at the end of his nose,
        His nose,
        His nose,
    With a ring at the end of his nose.

'Dear Pig, are you willing to sell for one shilling
    Your ring?' Said the Piggy, 'I will.'
So they took it away, and were married next day
    By the Turkey who lives on the hill.
They dined on mince, and slices of quince,
    Which they ate with a runcible spoon;
And hand in hand, on the edge of the sand,
    They danced by the light of the moon,
        The moon,
        The moon,
    They danced by the light of the moon.

221   Appearances

I

And so you found that poor room dull,
Dark, hardly to your taste, my dear ?
Its features seemed unbeautiful:
But this I know – 'twas there, not here,
You plighted troth to me, the word
Which–ask that poor room how it heard.

II

And this rich room obtains your praise
Unqualified,–so bright, so fair,
So all whereat perfection stays ?
Ay, but remember–here, not there,
The other word was spoken! Ask
This rich room how you dropped the mask.

222   *In a Gondola*

The moth's kiss, first!
Kiss me as if you made believe
You were not sure, this eve,
How my face, your flower, had pursed
Its petals up; so, here and there
You brush it, till I grow aware
Who wants me, and wide ope I burst.

The bee's kiss, now!
Kiss me as if you entered gay
My heart at some noonday,
A bud that dares not disallow
The claim, so all is rendered up,
And passively its shattered cup
Over your head to sleep I bow.

223   *Love In A Life*

Room after room,
I hunt the house through
We inhabit together.
Heart, fear nothing, for, heart, thou shalt find her –
Next time, herself! – not the trouble behind her
Left in the curtain, the couch's perfume!
As she brushed it, the cornice-wreath blossomed
                                    anew:
Yon looking-glass gleamed at the wave of her
                                  feather.

Yet the day wears,
And door succeeds door;
I try the fresh fortune –
Range from the wide house from the wing to
                                  the centre.
Still the same chance! she goes out as I enter.

Spend my whole day in the quest, – who cares?
But 'tis twilight, you see, – with such suites
                                        to explore,
Such closets to search, such alcoves to importune!

224   *Now*

Out of your whole life give but a moment!
All of your life that has gone before,
All to come after it, – so you ignore,
So you make perfect the present, – condense,
In a rapture of rage, for perfection's endowment,
Thought and feeling and soul and sense –
Merged in a moment which gives me at last
You around me for once, you beneath me, above me –
Me – sure that despite of time future, time past, –
This tick of our life-time's one moment you love me!
How long such suspension may linger? Ah, sweet –
The moment eternal -just that and no more –
When ecstasy's utmost we clutch at the core
While cheeks bum, arms open, eyes shut and lips meet!

225 *On the Death of Emily Jane Brontë*

My darling, thou wilt never know
The grinding agony of woe
   That we have borne for thee.
Thus may we consolation tear
E'en from the depth of our despair
   And wasting misery.

The nightly anguish thou art spared
When all the crushing truth is bared
   To the awakening mind,
When the galled heart is pierced with grief,
Till wildly it implores relief,
   But small relief can find.

Nor know'st thou what it is to lie
Looking forth with streaming eye
   On life's lone wilderness.
'Weary, weary, dark and drear,
How shall I the journey bear,
   The burden and distress?'

Then since thou art spared such pain
We will not wish thee here again;
   He that lives must mourn.
God help us through our misery
And give us rest and joy with thee
   When we reach our bourne!

226   *Love And Friendship*

Love is like the wild rose-briar,
Friendship like the holly-tree –
The holly is dark when the rose-briar blooms
But which will bloom most constantly?

The wild rose-briar is sweet in spring,
Its summer blossoms scent the air;
Yet wait till winter comes again
And who will call the wild-briar fair?

Then scorn the silly rose-wreath now
And deck thee with the holly's sheen,
That when December blights thy brow
He still may leave thy garland green.

227   *A Valentine*

I said to One I loved, 'Why art thou sad?'
   And he made answer, 'There hath been a tune
   Long floating round my brain; morn, night, and noon,
With inarticulate cadence making glad,
   Yet vexing me, because I could not find
   Words sweet enough to set to it, and bind
Its music round about my heart for aye.
Till, musing late above an ancient book,
   The window being open, breezes fleet
Lifted the rare old page, and sudden shook
   A loose leaf, writ with song, unto my feet:
In these quaint words me thought lies hid the key
   To all those cadences faint struggling round,
Now will I wed them to that melody,
   And set my Life to music by their sound;
E'en so I practised them upon my lute

Early and late, yet found they would not suit
  Together, though so sweet! and all the strain
Broke into discords! still the strain goes on,
But only angers me, its meaning gone;
  Nor will I ever seek to find it words again!'

228   *To Marguerite*

Yes! In the sea of life enisled,
    With echoing straits between us thrown,
Dotting the shoreless watery wild,
    We mortal millions live alone.
The islands feel the enclasping flow,
And then their endless bounds they know.

But when the moon their hollow lights,
    And they are swept by balms of spring,
And in their glens, on starry nights,
    The nightingales divinely sing;
And lovely notes, from shore to shore,
Across the sounds and channels pour –

Oh! then a longing like despair
    Is to their farthest caverns sent;
For surely once, they feel, we were
    Parts of a single continent!
Now round us spreads the watery plain –
Oh, might our marges meet again!

Who ordered that their longing's fire
    Should be, as soon as kindled, cooled?
Who renders vain their deep desire? –
    A God, a God their severance ruled!
And bade betwixt their shores to be
The unplumbed, salt, estranging sea.

229 *The Kiss*

'I saw you take his kiss!' ' 'Tis true.'
  'O, modesty!' ' 'Twas strictly kept:
'He thought me asleep; at least, I know
  'He thought I thought he thought I slept.'

230   *A Superscription*

Look in my face; my name is Might-have been;
　　I am also called No-more, Too-late, Farewell;
　　Unto thine ear I hold the dead-sea shell
Cast up thy life's foam-fretted feet between;
Unto thine eyes the glass where that is seen
　　Which had life's form and love's, but by my spell
　　Is now a shaken shadow intolerable,
Of ultimate things unuttered the frail screen.

Mark me, how still I am! But should there dart
　　One moment through thy soul the soft surprise
　　Of that winged peace which lulls the breath of sighs –
Then shalt thou see me smile, and turn apart
Thy visage to mine ambush at thy heart
　　Sleepless with cold commemorative eyes.

231 *Nuptial Sleep*

At length their long kiss severed, with sweet smart:
  And as the last slow sudden drops are shed
  From sparkling eaves when all the storm has fled,
So singly flagged the pulses of each heart.
Their bosoms sundered, with the opening start
  Of married flowers to either side outspread
  From the knit stem; yet still their mouths, burnt red,
Fawned on each other where they lay apart.

Sleep sank them lower than the tide of dreams,
  And their dreams watched them sink, and slid away.
Slowly their souls swam up again, through gleams
  Of watered light and dull drowned waifs of day;
  Till from some wonder of new woods and streams
He woke, and wondered more: for there she lay.

232   *Faraday's Discovery*

Around the magnet, Faraday
Is sure that Volta's lightnings play –
   But how to draw them from the wire?
He took a lesson from the heart
'Tis when we meet, 'tis when we part
   Breaks forth th'electric fire.

CHRISTINA ROSSETTI (1830–94)

233   A Birthday

My heart is like a singing bird
  Whose nest is in a watered shoot;
My heart is like an apple-tree
  Whose boughs are bent with thick-set fruit;
My heart is like a rainbow shell
  That paddles in a halcyon sea;
My heart is gladder than all these
  Because my love is come to me.

Raise me a daïs of silk and down;
  Hang it with vair and purple dyes;
Carve it in doves and pomegranates,
  And peacocks with a hundred eyes;
Work it in gold and silver grapes,
  In leaves and silver fleurs-de-lys;
Because the birthday of my life
  Is come, my love is come to me.

234   *The First Day*

I wish I could remember the first day,
First hour, first moment of your meeting me,
If bright or dim the season, it might be
Summer or Winter for aught that I can say;
So unrecorded did it slip away,
So blind was I to see and to foresee,
So dull to mark the budding of my tree
That would not blossom yet for many a May,
If only I could recollect it, such
A day of days! I let it come and go
As traceless as a thaw of bygone snow;
It seemed to mean so little, meant so much;
If only now I could recall that touch,
First touch of hand in hand. Did one but know!

CHRISTINA ROSSETTI

235 *Monna Innominata – IV*

I loved you first: but afterwards your love,
   Outsoaring mine, sang such a loftier song
As drowned the friendly cooings of my dove.
   Which owes the other most? My love was long,
   And yours one moment seemed to wax more strong;
I loved and guessed at you, you construed me
And loved me for what might or might not be –
   Nay, weights and measures do us both a wrong.
For verily love knows not 'mine' or 'thine';
With separate 'I' and 'thou' free love has done,
   For one is both and both are one in love:
Rich love knows nought of 'thine that is not mine';
   Both have the strength and both the length thereof,
Both of us, of the love which makes us one.

236 *Dead Love*

Oh never weep for love that's dead
Since love is seldom true
But changes his fashion from blue to red,
From brightest red to blue,
And love was born to an early death
And is so seldom true.

Then harbour no smile on your bonny face
To win the deepest sigh.
The fairest words on truest lips
Pass on and surely die, I
And you will stand alone, my dear,
When wintry winds draw nigh.

Sweet, never weep for what cannot be,
For this God has not given.
If the merest dream of love were true
Then, sweet, we should be in heaven,
And this is only earth, my dear,
Where true love is not given.

237   *Echoes of Love's House*

Love gives every gift whereby we long to live:
'Love takes every gift, and nothing back cloth give.'

Love unlocks the lips that else were ever dumb:
'Love locks up the lips whence all things good
                                        might come.'

Love makes clear the eyes that else would never see:
'Love makes blind the eyes to all but me and thee.'

Love turns life to joy till nought is left to gain:
'Love turns life to woe till hope is nought and vain.'

Love, who changest all, change me nevermore!
   'Love, who changest all, change my sorrow sore!'

Love burns up the world to changeless heaven
                           and blest,
'Love burns up the world to a void of all unrest.'

And there we twain are left, and no more work
                           we need.
'And I am left alone, and who my work shall heed?'

Ah! I praise thee, Love, for utter joyance won!
'And is my praise nought worth for all my
                           life undone?'

238 *Saragossa*

(*In Imitation of Thomas Moore*)

Pepita, my paragon, bright star of Arragon;
    Listen, dear, listen; your Cristobal sings.
From my cot that lies buried a short way from Lerida
    Love and a diligence lent me their wings.
Swift as a falcon I flew to thy balcony,
    (Is it bronchitis? I can't sing a bar.)
Greet not with merriment Love's first experiment;
    Listen, Pepita! I've brought my catarrh.

Manuel the matador may, like a flat, adore
    Donna Dolores: I pity his choice,
For they say that her governor lets neither lover nor
    Anyone else hear the sound of her voice.
Brother Bartolomé (stoutish Apollo) may
    Sigh for Sabina – you'll pardon this cough? –
And Isabel's votary, Nunez the notary,
    Vainly – (that sneeze again? Loved one, I'm Off!)

239   *Kissing Her Hair*

Kissing her hair I sat against her feet,
Wove and unwove it, wound and found it sweet;
Made last therewith her hands, drew down her eyes,
Deep as deep flowers and dreamy like dim skies;
With her own tresses bound and found her fair,
  Kissing her hair.

Sleep were no sweeter than her face to me,
Sleep of cold sea-bloom under the cold sea;
What pain could get between my face and hers?
What new sweet thing would love not relish worse?
Unless, perhaps, white death had kissed me there,
  Kissing her hair?

240 Tu Quoque

An Idyll in the Conservatory

NELLIE

If I were you, when ladies at the play, sir,
   Beckon and nod, a melodrama through,
I would not turn abstractedly away, sir,
   If I were you!

FRANK

If I were you, when persons I affected,
   Wait for three hours to take me down to Kew,
I would, at least, pretend I recollected,
   If I were you!

NELLIE

If I were you, when ladies are so lavish,
   Sir, as to keep me every waltz but two,
I would not dance with odious Miss M'Tavish
   If I were you!

FRANK

If I were you, who vow you cannot suffer
   Whiff of the best, the mildest 'honey-dew,'
I would not dance with smoke-consuming Puffer,
   If I were you!

NELLIE

If I were you, I would not, sir, be bitter,
   Even to write the Cynical Review; –

FRANK

No, I should doubtless find flirtation fitter,
   If I were you!

NELLIE

Really! You would? Why, Frank, you're quite delightful, –
   Hot as Othello, and as black of hue;
Borrow my fan. I would not look so frightful,
   If I were you!

FRANK

'It is the cause.' I mean your chaperon, is
   Bringing some well-curled juvenile. Adieu!
I shall retire. I'd spare that poor Adonis,
   If I were you!

Go, if you will. At once! And by express, sir!
  Where shall it be? To China – or Peru?
Go. I should leave inquirers my address, sir,
  If I were you!

No, – I remain. To stay and fight a duel
  Seems, on the whole, the proper thing to do –
Ah, you are strong, – I would not then be cruel,
  If I were you!

One does not like one's feelings to be doubted, –

One does not like one's friends to misconstrue, –

If I confess that I a wee-bit pouted? –

I should admit that I was piqué, too.

Ask me to dance. I'd say no more about it,
  If I were you!

241   *Farewell to Juliet*

I see you, Juliet, still, with your straw hat
Loaded with vines, and with your dear pale face,
On which those thirty years so lightly sat,
And the white outline of your muslin dress.
You wore a little fichu trimmed with lace
And crossed in front, as was the fashion then,
Bound at your waist with a broad band or sash.
All white and fresh and virginally plain.
There was a sound of shouting far away
Down in the valley, as they called to us,
And you, with hands clasped seeming still to pray
Patience of fate, stood listening to me thus
With heaving bosom. There a rose lay curled.
It was the reddest rose in all the world.

242   *A Church Romance*

She turned in the high pew, until her sight
Swept the west gallery, and caught its row
Of music-men with viol, book, and bow
Against the sinking sad tower-window light.

She turned again; and in her pride's despite
One strenuous viol's inspirer seemed to throw
A message from his string to her below,
Which said: 'I claim thee as my own forthright!'

Thus their hearts' bond began, in due time signed.
And long years thence, when Age had scared Romance,
At some old attitude of his or glance
That gallery-scene would break upon her mind,
   With him as minstrel, ardent, young, and trim,
   Bowing 'New Sabbath' or 'Mount Ephraim'.

243 *The End of the Episode*

Indulge no more may we
In this sweet-bitter pastime:
The love-light shines the last time
    Between you, Dear, and me.

There shall remain no trace
Of what so closely tied us,
And blank as ere love eyed us
    Will be our meeting-place.

The flowers and thymy air,
Will they now miss our coming?
The dumbles thin their humming
    To find we haunt not there?

Though fervent was our vow,
Though ruddily ran our pleasure,
Bliss has fulfilled its measure,
    And sees its sentence now.

Ache deep; but make no moans:
Smile out; but stilly suffer:
The paths of love are rougher
    Than thoroughfares of stones.

THOMAS HARDY

244   *I Look into My Glass*

I look into my glass,
And view my wasting skin,
And say, 'Would God it came to pass
My heart had shrunk as thin!'

For then, I, undistressed
By hearts grown cold to me,
Could lonely wait my endless rest
With equanimity.

But time, to make me grieve,
Part steals, lets part abide;
And shakes this fragile frame at eve
With throbbings of noontide.

245   *She Charged Me*

She charged me with having said this and that
To another woman long years before,
In the very parlour where we sat, –

Sat on a night when the endless pour
Of rain on the roof and the road below
Bent the spring of the spirit more and more . . .

– So charged she me; and the Cupid's bow
Of her mouth was hard, and her eyes, and her face,
And her white forefinger lifted slow.

Had she done it gently, or shown a trace
That not too curiously would she view
A folly flown ere her reign had place,

A kiss might have closed it. But I knew
From the fall of each word, and the pause between,
That the curtain would drop upon us two
Ere long, in our play of slave and queen.

JOHN BOYLE O'REILLY (1844–90)

246 *A White Rose*

The red rose whispers of passion,
　And the white rose breathes of love;
O, the red rose is a falcon,
　And the white rose is a dove.

But I send you a cream-white rosebud
　With a flush on its petal tips;
For the love that is purest and sweetest
　Has a kiss of desire on the lips.

247 Lost Love

Who wins his love shall lose her,
  Who lose her shall gain
For still the spirit woos her,
  A soul without a stain;
And memory still pursues her
  With longings not in vain!

He loses her who gains her,
  Who watches day by day
The dust of time that stains her,
  The griefs that leave her gray –
The flesh that yet enchains her
  Whose grace hath passed away!

Oh, happier he who gains not
    The love some seem to gain:
The joy that custom stains not
    Shall still with him remain;
The loveliness that wanes not,
    The love that ne'er can wane.

In dreams she grows not older
    The lands of dream among;
Though all the world wax colder,
    Though all the songs be sung,
In dreams doth he behold her
    Still fair and kind and young.

248 *O Joy of Love's Renewing*

O joy of love's renewing,
  Could love be born again;
Relenting for thy rueing,
  And pitying my pain:
O joy of love's awaking,
  Could love arise from sleep,
Forgiving our forsaking
  The fields we would not reap!

Fleet, fleet we fly, pursuing
  The love that fled amain,
But will he list our wooing,
  Or call we but in vain?
Ah! vain is all our wooing,
  And all our prayers are vain,
Love listeth not our suing,
  Love will not wake again.

249 *The Woods Are Still*

The woods are still that were so gay at
                              primrose-springing,
Through the dry woods the brown field-fares
                              are winging,
And I alone of love, of love am singing.

I sing of love to the haggard palmer-worm,
Of love 'mid the crumpled oak-leaves that once
                              were firm,
Laughing, I sing of love at the summer's term.

Of love, on a path where the snake's cast skin
                              is lying,
Blue feathers on the floor, and no cuckoo flying;
I sing to the echo of my own voice crying.

250   *The Garden*

My heart shall be thy garden. Come my own
Into thy garden; thine be happy hours
Among my fairest thoughts, my tallest flowers,
From root to crowning petal thine alone.

Thine is the place, from where the seeds are sown
Up to the sky enclosed, with all its showers.
But ah, the birds, the birdst Who shall build bowers
To keep these thine? O friend, the birds have flown.

For as these come and go, and quit our pine
To follow the sweet season, or, newcomers,
Sing one song only from our alder-trees,

My heart has thoughts, which, though thine eyes
                                  hold mine,
Flit to the silent world and other summers,
With wings that dip beyond the silver seas.

251 Renouncement

I must not think of thee; and, tired yet strong,
I shun the thought that lurks in all delight –
The thought of thee – and in the blue heaven's height,
And in the sweetest passage of a song.
O just beyond the fairest thoughts that throng
This breast, the thought of thee waits, hidden yet bright;
But it must never, never come in sight;
I must stop short of thee the whole day long.
But when sleep comes to close each difficult day,
When night gives pause to the long watch I keep,
And all my bonds I needs must loose apart,
And doff my will as raiment laid away, –
With the first dream that comes with the first sleep,
I run, I run, I am gathered to thy heart.

252   *Without Him*

Senza te son nulla – PETRARCH

I touched the heart that loved me, as a player
   Touches a lyre; content with my poor skill
   No touch save mine knew my belov'd (and still
I thought at times: Is there no sweet lost air
Old loves could wake in him, I cannot share?);
   Oh, he alone, alone could so fulfil,
   My thoughts in sound, to the measure of my will.
He is dead, and silence takes me unawares.

The songs I knew not he resumes, set free
From my constraining love, alas for me!
   His part in our tune goes with him; my part
I locked in me for ever; I stand as mute
   As one with full strung music in his heart
Whose ringers stray upon a shattered lute.

253 'No, Thank You, Tom'

They met, when they were girl and boy,
   Going to school one day,
And, 'Won't you take my peg-top, dear?'
   Was all that he could say.
She bit her little pinafore,
   Close to his side she came;
She whispered, 'No! no, thank you, Tom,'
   But took it all the same.

They met one day, the selfsame way,
   When ten swift years had flown;
He said, 'I've nothing but my heart,
   But that is yours alone;
And won't you take my heart?' he said,
   And called her by her name;
She blushed, and said, 'No, thank you, Tom,'
   But took it all the same.

And twenty, thirty, forty years
    Have brought them care and joy;
She has the little peg-top still
    He gave her when a boy.
'I've had no wealth, sweet wife,' says he,
    'I've never brought you fame; '
She whispers, 'No! no, thank you, Tom,
    You've loved me all the same!'

254   *I Will Make You Brooches*

I will make you brooches and toys for your delight
Of bird-song at morning and star-shine at night.
I will make a palace fit for you and me,
Of green days in forests and blue days at sea.

I will make my kitchen, and you shall keep your room,
Where white flows the river and bright blows the broom,
And you shall wash your linen and keep your body white
In rainfall at morning and dewfall at night.

And this shall be for music when no one else is near,
The fine song for singing, the rare song to hear!
That only I remember, that only you admire,
Of the broad road that stretches and the roadside fire.

255 *A Valediction*

If we must part,
Then let it he like this;
Not heart on heart,
Nor with the useless anguish of a kiss;
But touch mine hand and say:
'Until to-morrow or some other day,
If we must part.'

Words are so weak
When love hath been so strong:
Let silence speak.
'Life is a little while, and love is long;
A time to sow and reap,
And after harvest a long time to sleep,
But words are weak.'

256   *Love's Ways*

You were not cruel always! Nay,
　　When I said Come! one year ago:
Could you have lingered by the way?
　　Did not the very wind seem slow?

Then, had you tarried, I had known
　　Nor love's delight, nor lost love's pain:
Then, always had I lived alone.
　　Now, you need never come again.

AMY LOWELL (1874–1925)

257   *The Taxi*

When I go away from you
The world beats dead
Like a slackened drum.
I call out for you against the jutted stars
And shout into the ridges of the wind.
Streets coming fast,
One after the other,

Wedge you away from me,
And the lamps of the city prick my eyes
So that I can no longer see your face.
Why should I leave you,
To wound myself upon the sharp edges
                                    of the night?

(GLADYS) MARY WEBB (1881–1927)

258   *My Love Is in the Mountains*

My Love is in the mountains dark and high,
Where winds lie dead beneath an icy sky;
Where only the cold stars are intimate;
And tears are frozen in falling and voices die.

How shall I ever climb where my Love is,
Out of life's small and bright miscellanies,
To the unsullied mountains desolate –
From silences to deeper silences?

From the red tilth and the warm woods I go
Upward, and leave the meadows dear and low;
Seeing afar, when the cold hours grow late,
My Love amid the hills of silver snow.

259   *Very Early*

Very early we will go into the fields tomorrow
And wait beneath the budding elm tree arches,
Till Earth has comforted her night-long sorrow
And dawn comes golden in the larches.

There's a little hush that falls when the airs lie sleeping;
The sky is like an empty silver bowl,
Till eagerly the blackbird's song goes upward sweeping,
And fills the aery hollows, and the soul.

There's a scent that only comes in the faint, fresh gloaming,
Before the crocus opens for the bees;
So early we will go and meet the young day roaming,
And see the heavens caught among the trees.

260 *Why?*

Why did you come, with your enkindled eyes
And mountain-look, across my lower way.
And take the vague dishonour from my day
By luring me from paltry things, to rise
And stand beside you, waiting wistfully
The looming of a larger destiny?

Why did you with strong fingers fling aside
The gates of possibility, and say
With vital voice the words I dream today?
Before, I was not much unsatisfied:
But since a god has touched me and departed,
I run through every temple, broken-hearted.

261   *In January*

What shall I tell thee of?
Of the new sad memories one name can move?
Of the Heaven that Love brings? or of the Hell
That followed such Love?
Of these shall I tell?

I have not forgotten yet
The mist that shrouded all things, cold and wet;
The dripping bough: the sad smell of the rotten
Leaves. How should I forget?
Hast thou forgotten?

Dost thou remember now
How our eyes met; and all things changed; and how
A glorious light thrilled all that dim December,
And a bird sang on the bough?
Dost thou remember?

262   Love

Love is a breach in the walls, a broken gate,
  Where that comes in that shall not go again;
Love sells the proud heart's citadel to Fate.
  They have known shame, who love unloved.
                                    Even then
When two mouths, thirsty each for each, find slaking,
  And agony's forgot, and hushed the crying
Of credulous hearts, in heaven-such are but taking
  Their own poor dreams within their arms, and lying
Each in his lonely night, each with a ghost.
  Some share that night. But they know, love
                                    grows colder,
Grows false and dull, that was sweet lies at most.
  Astonishment is no more in hand or shoulder,
But darkens, and dies out from kiss to kiss.
All this is love; and all love is but this.

263 Oh! Death Will Find Me

Oh! death will find me, long before I tire
   Of watching you; and swing me suddenly
Into the shade and loneliness and mire
   Of the last land! There, waiting patiently,
One day, I think, I'll feel a cool wind blowing,
   See a slow light across the Stygian tide,
And hear the dead about me stir, unknowing,
   And tremble. And I shall know that you have died.
And watch you, a broad-browed and smiling dream,
   Pass, light as ever, through the lightless host,
Quietly ponder, start, and sway, and gleam –
   Most individual and bewildering ghost! –
And turn, and toss your brown delightful head
Amusedly, among the ancient dead.

264   *There's Wisdom in Women*

'Oh love is fair, and love is rare;' my dear one she said,
'But love goes lightly over.' I bowed her foolish head,
And kissed her hair and laughed at her. Such a
                                    child was she;
So new to love, so true to love, and she spoke so bitterly.

But there's wisdom in women, of more than they
                                    have known,
And thoughts go blowing through them, are wiser
                                    than their own,
Or how should my dear one, being ignorant and young
Have cried on love so bitterly, with so true a tongue?

PETER ARTHUR (1915–2000)

265 *Lunch-Time Drinks*

People I knew, a crowd
   in the high-ceilinged room,
   an airbag of noise
   and the drinks winking
   in the mid-day light;
   and I was at ease.

Then suddenly she was there
   close beside me, hemmed in
   by the crush, young, small,
   in a pale mauve dress.

I did not recognise her,
   but knew who she was
   by the stab of longing
   that caught me unawares.

She looked up at me smiling,
    merging all her several smiles,
    and we were alone – island
    in an inconsequential sea –
    our future out beyond
    over the sun-lit lawn.

266   *Old Man Dreaming*

Black girl –
smooth black skin great
dark eyes dreadlocked
jet black hair, your
slim young five-foot
form fine-boned broad
nosed and sculpted
face, you are child to me.

But so and with your good
two-one, your poise
dress sense high-tech
flair know how and
air of cultured
competence, I
would be mighty
scared of you.

And yet –
seems that I would
dearly love to
lie with you and
feel your warmth and
smell your strange
exotic smell and
kiss those rose-red
dusky lips.

267   *Power cut*

Quietly
We sit in the Aga-warmth
Of the kitchen.
Soft saffron candlelight
Flickers ancient shadows;
Old forgotten household
Noises deepen the unlooked for
Silence.

We wait,
Speaking sometimes, softly
In the measured stillness.
No duty calls to action,
Nothing compels us now;
All is quiet, at rest,
Unstressed.

Alone
In the soft yellow candle-glow
We smile, gently touching
Hands across the deal table;
Eyes meet, there is peace, tranquility.
We wait expectantly, without fear,
Trusting.

268   *May: for Margaret*

I watch you smile for these pale fable-bearers
who brighten in the passing wake of shadow
pitched by a sun which sets the garden flying.
Their proper, common names, shrouded in green,
lie quiet as black loam, as alluvial pebbles
dull with earth-glow, as husky stems that die back
into a stump-work of clay and cobbles.

Today, the calendar brings round your name-day,
a year pared to the quick – Maius, Magius,
whose root signifies new growth. Sap rising:
the copse hemmed in, stitched-up by Queen
                                        Anne's Lace,
Cow-Parsley, Gipsy's Curtain, Lady's Needlework.
Our late paths close to one dark runnelling
through the rough, heady scent, as moonlight

bares this, the frailest of those English ghosts,
whose long processional canopies nod by
hooding their soldier-beetles, forkytails:
Hedge-Parsley, Hemlock, Hogweed, Alexander.
all keep their simple virtues, reach for light
with a green darkness piping through their stems:
Puck's Needle, Devils' Nightcap, Bad Man's Oatmeal,

and, stronger for culling on the orchard floor,
not yet Dog-Daisy of the long dog-days —
the Moon's Eye, Mowing Daisy of high summer —
but Bellis Perennis, La Belle Marguerite,
The Pearl, the Eye of Day, her white-and-red
wearing your name, the shadow of your substance,
the substance of your shadow: mortal flesh.

269 *Audience Song*

Let's give three cheers for Mother Nature
And some more for good old Mr Sun –
Hurrah! For the plants that take our CO_2
And convert it back to oxygen for me and you
So three hearty cheers for Mother Nature
And the Moon and the Stars above
And let's be truly thankful
For the chemical reactions
That make us fall in love.

270 *Aurora*

I came to my love in the early morn
And she lay on her back and opened her lips
And the birds all sang in chorus at dawn.

I came to my love in the afternoon
The sky deep blue, there were clouds like ships,
Butterflies, larks, and an ice-cold moon.

I came to my love in the dead of night
In absolute darkness my finger tips
Guided my love with unerring sight.

Alphabetical list of Authors

Alexander, Sir William,
    Earl of Stirling,
Arnold, Matthew
Arthur, Peter

Baillie, Joanna
Barker, Jane
Behn, Aphra
Best, Charles
Blacklock, Thomas
Blake, William
Blunt, Wilfrid
Bradstreet, Anne
Breton, Nicholas
Brome, Alexander
Brontë, Charlotte
Brontë, Emily

Brooke, Rupert
Browning, Elizabeth
    Barrett
Browning, Robert
Burns, Robert
Burrell, Sophia
Byron, Lord

Campion, Thomas
Carew, Thomas
Cavendish, William, Duke
    of Newcastle
Clare, John
Cockburn, Catherine
Coleridge, Samuel Taylor
Constable, Henry
Cowper, William

Kemble, Fanny

Lang, Andrew
Langland, William
Lear, Edward
Lee, Nathaniel
Leigh, H. S.
Lennox, Charlotte
Littleton, Edward
Lodge, Thomas
Lovelace, Richard
Lowell, Amy
Lyly, John

Mabbe, James
Margaret, Duchess of
    Newcastle,
Marlowe, Christopher
Marvell, Andrew
Meynell, Alice
Middleton, Thomas

Montagu, Lady Mary
    Wortley
Moore, Thomas
Morris, William

Norton, Caroline

O'Keefe, John
O'Reilly, John Boyle
Otway, Thomas

Parnell, Thomas
Patmore, Coventry
Peele, George
Philips, Ambrose
Philips, Katherine
Pilkington, Laetitia
Prior, Matthew

Quarles, Francis
Queen Elizabeth I

Index of first lines

Ev'ning, now, from purple wings 151

Farewell, Love, and all thy laws forever 7
Farewell, sweet Love! Yet blame you not my truth 188
Farewell! thou art too dear for my possessing 51
First time he kissed me, he but only kissed 213
For love's sake, kiss me once again! 60
Forbear, bold youth, all's Heaven here 117

Give me, my love, that billing kiss 194
Go from me. Yet I feel that I shall stand 206
Golden slumbers kiss your eyes 70

Had we but world enough, and time 114
Hail, happy bride, for thou art truly blest! 148
He that loves a rosy cheek 95
Her eyes the glow-worm lend thee 81
Here lies a nymph! Whose beauty was her bane 169
How do I love thee? Let me count the ways 214
How love came in, I do not know 83

My Infelice's face, her brow, her eye 72
My little lady I may not leave behind 6
My love is as a fever, longing still 55
My Love is in the mountains dark and high 258
My love is of a birth as rare 113
My mistress' eyes are nothing like the sun 53
My true love hath my heart and I have his 25

Never seek to tell thy love 173
No longer mourn for me when I am dead 50
Nor marble, nor the gilded monuments 49
Not, Celia, that I juster am 122
Now sleeps the crimson petal, now the white 217

O faithless world, and thy most faithless part 58
O joy of love's renewing 248
O love, how thou art tired out with rhyme! 115
O love is so deceiving 199
O Love! what art thou, Love? the ace of hearts 202
O lovers' eyes are sharp to see 185

This edition first published in 2003 by
Book Blocks an imprint of
CRW Publishing Limited
69 Gloucester Crescent, London NW1 7EG

ISBN 1 904633 19 6

Typeset in Great Britain by Antony Gray
Printed and bound in China

This edition first published in 2003 by
Book Blocks an imprint of
CRW Publishing Limited
69 Gloucester Crescent, London NW1 7EG

ISBN 1 904633 19 6

Typeset in Great Britain by Antony Gray
Printed and bound in China